STEAM LOCOMOTIVES 1955

1-39999

WESTERN AND SOUTHERN

No. 3012 from Pontypool Road depot, South Wales, had obviously failed at Oxford as it was standing in the yard with two 'Not to be moved' signs on the locomotive buffer beam. Only a few of these powerful locomotives still remained in service in the mid-fifties.

31.10.54

STEAM LOCOMOTIVES 1955

1–39999
WESTERN
AND SOUTHERN

ERIC SAWFORD

ALAN SUTTON PUBLISHING LIMITED

First published in the United Kingdom in 1996
Alan Sutton Publishing Ltd · Phoenix Mill · Far Thrupp · Stroud · Gloucestershire

British Library Cataloguing in Publication Data

Sawford, E.H.
    Steam Locomotives, 1955. – 1–39999
    Western and Southern
    I. Title
    625.2610942

ISBN 0-7509-1002-X

Title page picture: 'County' class no. 1026 *County of Salop* at Old Oak Common depot, its home shed when this picture was taken. By the mid-fifties no 'Counties' were allocated to this depot.
9.9.51

Typeset in 10/12 Palatino.
Typesetting and origination by
Alan Sutton Publishing Limited.
Printed in Great Britain by
Butler & Tanner, Frome, Somerset.

Contents

Introduction

There were many veteran locomotives still at work on British Railways in 1955 and, of the two regions covered in this volume, it was the Southern that had the most interesting, such as the aged Beattie 2–4–0 'Well' tanks at Wadebridge and the graceful Adams 4–4–2 tanks on the Lyme Regis branch. The Western Region had benefited from the Great Western policy of standardization of locomotive designs, although as with all general rules there were exceptions and among these were the few remaining ex-Welsh Railways tank locomotives.

The two regions covered a large proportion of the country. The Southern, with several London termini, covered south of the River Thames and across into Devon and Cornwall, and the Western from Paddington covered the West Country, South and Mid-Wales and the West Midlands. Western Region engines also reached the London Midland stronghold of Crewe. One of the principal expresses out of Paddington was the prestigious ' The Cornish Riviera', usually headed by a 'King' class on the first stage and 'County' or 'Castle' class from Plymouth to Penzance.

In 1955 very few main line diesel locomotives were in service, steam power having almost complete monopoly. On the Western Region the principal express passenger locomotives were the 'King' class 4–6–0s introduced by Collett in 1927 and the very useful 'Castle' class, the last of which had been delivered just five years earlier in 1950. Those who can remember these times at Paddington will doubtless recall the steady stream of arrivals and departures of these fine locomotives with their immaculate paintwork and gleaming brass and copper fittings.

The once familiar 'Saint' class locomotives had all been withdrawn at this time and the very few remaining examples of the 'Stars' were mostly to be seen in the West Midlands. There were 329 examples of the 'Hall' and later 'Modified Hall' 4–6–0s in service. These engines were certainly no strangers to Paddington and were to be found on main lines throughout the region with a few exceptions such as the Cambrian. Many of the 'Modified Halls' had been in service just a few years as a considerable number of them were delivered in British Railways days. These engines were introduced in 1944 to a Hawksworth design, and were a development of the 'Hall' class with larger superheater, one piece main frames and a bogie of plate frame construction. The 'Halls' were officially classified as a mixed traffic design and the 'Granges', a variation of the class with smaller driving wheels, came into the same group. These were often seen heading fast freight and were also extensively used on passenger workings especially in the West Country.

In 1919 Churchward introduced his 4700 class 2–8–0s. This nine-strong class was principally for fast freight services, although on numerous occasions they found themselves on passenger duties. With a tractive effort almost equal to the 'Castles' they were ideal for use on specials and excursions. Seven of the class were allocated to Old Oak Common in the mid-fifties and the other two to Bristol St Phillips Marsh.

Both regions relied very heavily on mixed traffic locomotives of the 4–6–0 wheel arrangement; the Western had several designs, the Hall and Modified Hall classes alone amounting to 329 locomotives. No. 4938 *Liddington Hall* is pictured here at Oxford.

31.10.54

Each region had its 'Maids of all work' and on the Western this title fitted admirably the 'Mogul' 2–6–0s. Although their numbers were slowly declining with withdrawals of the earlier engines, they were still to be found throughout the region with more than two hundred in service on a wide range of duties.

On the Great Western the 0–6–0 tender design was not generally as common as elsewhere in the country. The famous 'Dean Goods' of the 2301 class were down to the last few examples and other classes of the wheel arrangement taken over at the grouping had disappeared, leaving just the 2251 class of 120 locomotives which first made their appearance in 1930, with the last being delivered in 1948. These were very useful engines and many depots had examples of the design in their allocations including Old Oak Common which had four members of the class. The 'Dean Goods' mentioned earlier were withdrawn in large numbers during the early fifties and the sad sight of long rows of these engines awaiting cutting up could be seen at Swindon Works.

Heavy goods traffic on the Western was the domain of Churchward's 2800 class introduced in 1903. Shortly before the Second World War delivery of a second batch commenced and the last was completed in 1942. One of the improvements was the fitting of side window cabs, no doubt welcomed by the enginemen, and other detail alterations were also included. For handling short haul heavy mineral traffic large tank locomotives were favoured, the 4200 class 2–8–0Ts first appearing to a Churchward design in 1910. As with the tender engines improvements were made. These later engines were known as the 5205 class and had larger cylinders, higher tractive effort and other detail differences. In 1923 a decision was made by Collett to rebuild some of these engines as 2–8–2Ts with extended bunkers which in the process added ten tons to their weight. In all fifty-four engines were rebuilt, becoming the 7200 class. By far the largest concentration of the 4200 and 7200 classes was in South Wales although a few examples were to be found at other depots.

Nearing the end of their days at this time were the ROD class engines. These very versatile locomotives were of a Robinson Great Central design. With the need for engines to work in France and other countries during the First World War this very rugged and well proven design was chosen for new production for the War Department. After the cessation of hostilities vast quantities of all types of equipment became available for purchase. The Great Western eventually acquired a hundred of these engines, the first being taken into stock in 1919. Despite the addition of Great Western fittings they never lost the unmistakable outline of the Great Central design. By the mid-fifties their numbers had been reduced to just a handful, the last survivor soldiering on until 1958.

Suburban services in the London area were in the hands of the 6100 class. These were introduced for this work in 1931 and were very successful, powerful engines capable of a fair turn of speed. The majority of the class were allocated to the Old Oak Common district but eventually they were displaced by more modern motive power and became much more widely distributed.

Local passenger services in other parts of the region were often worked by 5100 class locomotives and a modified design, introduced for new construction from 1929, known as the 5101 class. Another much smaller class was the 8100, the ten engines being rebuilds of the 5100 class with smaller wheels.

Many rural branch and cross country lines were still in operation although their days were numbered. Before the next decade many had closed and isolated communities had to rely solely on road transport. One of the early Western Region casualties was the Yelverton to Princetown branch. This line crossing the moors was for years the domain of the 4400 class 2–6–2Ts.

The Great Western also made extensive use of the Auto train. One class of locomotive designed for this work was the 1400 class 0–4–2Ts. These nippy little engines with their auto coach were a familiar sight on many Western Region branches. They were not, however, the only classes equipped for this work as the 5400 and 6400 classes were also push-pull fitted. All three designs were introduced by Collett in the early thirties.

One other type of locomotive favoured by the chief mechanical engineers of the Great Western and Western Region shortly after nationalization was the 'Pannier' tank. The most numerous was undoubtedly the 5700 class, introduced in 1929, with 863 examples in service during the mid-fifties. They were to be seen on many duties such as shunting work, light goods and local passenger. Those equipped with condensing gear worked over the Metropolitan line. After withdrawal several of these engines were to have a second lease of life with London Transport and the National Coal Board.

There were several other pannier tank designs dating from GWR days: the 5400 and 6400 classes mentioned previously, the 7400 class similar to the 6400s but not push-pull fitted and the six examples of the 1361 class, several of which were a familiar sight on the quays at Weymouth. Shortly before nationalization Hawksworth introduced his powerful, taper boiler 9400 class locomotives which were designed for heavy shunting work. After nationalization, he also introduced the 1600 class for branch line and general shunting duties and the ten examples of the 1500 class with their short wheelbase. For a time these were to be seen at Paddington on empty stock workings.

In 1938 the first of the 'Manor' class emerged from Swindon Works and these 4–6–0s were designed for work on secondary lines. One feature of this class was that certain parts used were from withdrawn 'Moguls'. One area where the class excelled was on the Cambrian until more modern locomotives in the form of Standard class 4MT 4–6–0s were transferred for use on the line.

At the end of the working day a number of pannier tanks await their turn for coaling and watering at Bristol St Phillips Marsh depot. Heading the line is 9400 class no. 8491, one of several examples of this design allocated to the depot.

31.8.55

For many years this line was also the 'stamping ground' of the 9000 class, a 4–4–0 design introduced in 1936. They were known as 'Dukedogs'; this was hardly surprising as they incorporated 'Duke of Cornwall' type boilers and frames from members of the 'Bulldog' class. These locomotives had outside frames and a tall chimney which gave them a very dated appearance. They were technically new engines but were in fact very much reconstructions. During the early fifties no less than fourteen of the total of twenty-six were to be found at Machynlleth and a further three at Oswestry. One, no. 9015, was allocated to Oxford although on the several occasions when I visited the shed it was always present in the yard.

During the early fifties visitors to South Wales could find a variety of locomotives originating from Welsh railway companies later absorbed into the Great Western. By 1955 their numbers had dwindled to a mere handful and it was only a matter of a year or so before some of those remaining became extinct. Among these were the ex-Taff Vale Railway 0–6–2Ts. The remaining survivors were to be found in the Cardiff area, as were the ex-Rhymney Railway 0–6–2Ts. Some of the ex-Welsh locomotives gained a short reprieve on arrival at Swindon Works, where they were employed shunting locomotives before they also joined the sad line on the Swindon scrap road.

Unlike the other regions the Western had a few narrow gauge locomotives in normal service. The London Midland also had engines of other gauges all of which were engaged in departmental work at various works and depots. The Western had three 1 ft 11½ in gauge 2–6–2Ts, the 'Vale of Rheidol' locomotives, and the two Welshpool & Llanfair 0–6–0Ts. The latter line closed in November 1956.

4

Shunting work in dock areas usually required short wheelbase 0–4–0 tank locomotives and the Western had a selection of these. The most modern were the six examples of the 1101 class 0–4–0Ts built by the Avonside Engine Company in Bristol especially for Great Western requirements and introduced in 1926. Other interesting engines were the 0–4–0STs which came to the GWR from Powlesland & Mason contractors and the 0–4–0Ts once owned by the Swansea Harbour Trust. All the standard gauge locomotives of the Cambrian Railway, Brecon & Merthyr and several other small companies had been withdrawn by the mid-fifties, many shortly after nationalization.

There was more variation among the locomotives of the Southern Region. Even among the larger classes such as the 'King Arthurs' there were several variations and this variety extended through many designs right down to the smaller tank locomotives.

The pride of the Southern locomotive fleet were the Bulleid Pacifics. In the mid-fifties the thirty-strong 'Merchant Navy' class still had examples awaiting rebuilding and the lightweight Pacifics of the 'West Country' and 'Battle of Britain' classes were also undergoing a rebuilding programme although many of these ended their days still in unrebuilt form. During the early fifties the Pacific designs were to be seen on the Eastern section with the 'Merchant Navy' class working the highly prestigious 'Golden Arrow' and other boat trains, joined later by Britannia Pacifics. Kent coast electrification displaced many of these engines, nevertheless they performed excellent work on Weymouth, Bournemouth and other services until the end of steam on the Southern Region.

The 'Lord Nelson' and 'King Arthur' classes were not as frequently seen on expresses as more Bulleid Pacifics were delivered. In due course many of these locomotives were to find themselves on semi–fast services. The N15X 'Remembrance' class 4–6–0s ended their days working similar duties from Basingstoke.

Prior to electrification most of the heavy boat trains from the Kent ports were worked by Bulleid Pacifics. No. 34078 *222 Squadron* is shown here heading for London through Folkestone Central with a boat train.

28.6.53

The Southern had several classes of 4–4–0 tender locomotives, with examples from the London and South Western, South Eastern and Chatham and the last of the 4–4–0s originating from the London Brighton and South Coast being withdrawn shortly after nationalization. Certainly among the most attractive locomotive designs of this wheel arrangement were the Wainwright D & E classes introduced by the South Eastern and Chatham in 1901 and 1905 respectively. In both cases a few engines had been rebuilt completely changing their appearance. The rebuilds became classes D1 and E1 and these engines were frequently seen on Kent coast express services in the early fifties. The London and South Western Railway had introduced quite a number of 4–4–0 designs over the years and by the mid-fifties only a few D15 class and the very useful T9s remained. These latter engines were extensively used in the South West working on such duties as the Padstow branch. They were also to be found at Nine Elms where they often worked parcels and perishable traffic.

The Southern introduced the famous 'Schools' class in 1930 to a Maunsell design, these three cylinder engines becoming the V class. The 'Schools' were the last new locomotives of this wheel arrangement to be introduced in this country. Forty engines were constructed between 1930 and 1935, all of which were named after famous schools. The class was to be found on many parts of the Southern Region with the exception of the South West. Some engines were fitted with multiple jet blastpipes and larger chimneys although this did little to improve their appearance.

Goods traffic in the region was in the hands of the S15 class 4–6–0s, a development of the 'King Arthurs' for mixed traffic work, and the 2–6–0 classes of K, N, N1, U and U1. Local freight duties were handled by the thirty examples of the 700 class introduced by Drummond for the London and South Western in 1897 and the C class, a Wainwright design for the South Eastern and Chatham. Originating from London Brighton and South Coast days were the C2X class engines introduced in 1908 by Marsh. There were also several other smaller classes: the O1s with the outside framed tenders, the Qs introduced in 1938 by Maunsell and the 0395 class veterans dating back to 1881. The Bulleid 'Austerity' 0–6–0s of the Q1 class certainly caused a stir when they appeared in 1942 with their unconventional appearance. They were powerful engines with 5 ft 1 in driving wheels and a tractive effort of 30,080 lbs. In all forty were built.

Two classes which have now unfortunately become just memories are the 4–6–2Ts of the H16 class which Urie introduced to the London and South Western for heavy freight traffic and his 'hump' shunting 4–8–0T design of class G16. Five and four engines respectively were built to these designs and all were allocated to Feltham depot in the mid-fifties.

By this time only a few examples of the Marsh-designed 'Brighton Atlantics' remained in service. These engines were very similar to the Ivatt Atlantics of Great Northern Railway origin which I had seen in action on the East Coast main line. Fortunately, on the two occasions when I visited Brighton shed one was present. No. 32424 *Beachy Head* was the last Atlantic locomotive to run in normal service and was withdrawn in 1958.

Also at Brighton at this time was 'Terrier' 377S, the Brighton works shunter, resplendent in the London Brighton and South Coast yellow livery. In 1959 this engine returned to normal service stock as no. 32635. 'Terriers' were allocated to Fratton depot and used on the Hayling Island branch.

One of the most numerous tank designs in use on the Southern Region was the E4 class 0–6–2Ts introduced by R.J. Billinton to the London Brighton and South Coast in 1910. He also introduced the E3 and E2 classes, the former in 1894 and the ten examples of the latter in 1913.

The E1 class 0–6–0Ts were a much earlier design dating from Stroudley days and first making their appearance in 1874. They were later reboiled by Marsh and several were still in use, some at Eastleigh and Southampton Docks and four others, numbered W1–4 and all named, on the Isle of Wight. The 1927 Maunsell rebuilds of the E1 class to an 0–6–2T design were for passenger service in the West Country and classified E1/R.

At the other end of the scale were the small 0–6–0T tank locomotives of the P class originally designed for push-pull work and for some time relegated to light shunting duties. One of the spectacular sights of steam power was provided by the R1 class 0–6–0Ts working on the Folkestone Harbour branch. To work a heavy boat train up to Folkestone Junction required no less than four locomotives, three at the front and a fourth banking. The engines opened up as they crossed the swing bridge immediately after they left the harbour station. Nearly all the remaining examples of this Stirling 1888 design for the South Eastern Railway were allocated to Folkestone Junction, a sub-shed of Dover. The exceptions were those fitted with short Urie-type chimneys modified for use on the Whitstable branch. Also still in service were a few G6 class 0–6–0Ts of London and South Western design.

The Southern made considerable use of 0–4–4Ts with classes coming from several of the pre-grouping railways. The H class was a 1904 Wainwright design for the South Eastern and Chatham and many of these were converted in British Railways days for push-pull working. Apart from the E1 class, the other class responsible for handling most of the Isle of Wight's passenger services, which incidentally were much more extensive

The R1 class 0–6–0Ts at Folkestone shed had very demanding work: it was their responsibility to haul the heavy boat trains up from the Harbour station to Folkestone Junction where a larger locomotive waited to work the train forward to London. No. 31107 and a classmate await their next duty.

3.7.53

than at present, was the O2 class 0–4–4Ts. They were all named and of London and South Western origin. Other examples of the class were to be found in use on the mainland. Another very numerous class, which also was a London and South Western design, was the M7 0–4–4Ts. These were introduced by Drummond in 1897 and several were push-pull fitted. They were used on many duties including branch lines and carriage pilots. Examples of the class were still to be seen at Clapham Junction in the early sixties.

For many years the B4 class 0–4–0Ts had been a familiar sight at Southampton Docks. They were replaced by the 0–6–0 USA tanks which the Southern purchased from the US Army Transportation Corps in 1946. These were fitted with a modified bunker, cab and other detail alterations and took over most of the duties on the docks with the surviving B4 class locomotives being distributed to a number of depots. The other 0–4–0T on the Southern Region was the C14 class, the three members being nos. 30588/9 and no. 77S in service stock. The first two were employed on shunting work at Southampton Quay and allocated to Eastleigh depot.

At the start of this introduction I briefly mentioned the Lyme Regis 4–4–2Ts and the Beattie 2–4–0 tanks to be found at Wadebridge. During the fifties many enthusiasts visited these two branches and as a result the locomotives were frequently recorded on film and cine. The Lyme Regis Adams 4–4–2Ts were a graceful design, the three remaining examples numbered 30582–4 having long outlived their classmates. One of these had been sold to the Government in 1917, eventually passing into the ownership of the East Kent Railway before being re–acquired by the Southern Railway in 1946. Normal traffic on the branch was handled by one engine but on busy summer Saturdays two could often be seen double heading on this steeply graded line. Many holiday-makers travelled by rail to Lyme Regis in those days.

Down on the North Cornwall coast the three Beattie 'Well' 2–4–0Ts, designated 0298 class, were still at work on the Wenford Bridge mineral line operating from Wadebridge depot. These were first introduced in 1874 and rebuilt on several occasions over the years. They long outlived their classmates as all the other engines of this type were withdrawn prior to 1898. The three engines normally operated on a two in steam basis, covering the branch and shunting duties, with the third kept usually in the shed as a spare engine. There were exceptions of course when one of the engines was receiving works attention or under repair. My one and only visit to Wadebridge when these engines were still at work was in heavy rain but fortunately I managed to record all three on film.

Many of the classes mentioned have representatives in preservation. This is due in no small part to the many Western and Southern engines which were sent to Barry scrapyard from where they were purchased for preservation, often after years of exposure to the salt-laden atmosphere and in very different condition to when they arrived.

For many years the historic 3700 'City' class GWR no. 3717 *City of Truro* has been preserved. This engine is reputed to have reached 100 m.p.h. in 1904 heading a Plymouth to Paddington 'Ocean Mails Special'. *City of Truro* was overhauled and restored to full working order as no. 3440 and for a number of years worked on main lines and on preserved railways. It is seen here on the Severn Valley Railway. The locomotive is part of the National Collection at York Railway Museum.

Finally the Western and Southern Regions had very different methods of classifying and numbering their locomotives. As the book covers both, the order is firstly based on locomotive wheel arrangements, tender engines followed by tank classes in each region, with the individual classes in numerical or alphabetical order as appropriate under each section.

Eric Sawford

The historic 3700 'City' class GWR no. 3717 *City of Truro*.

28.9.85

1000 'County' class 4–6–0 6MT

These mixed traffic locomotives were introduced by the Great Western Railway in 1945.
Designer: F.W. Hawksworth.
Total built: 30, 1945–7.

Principal dimensions

Weight:	Locomotive	76 tons 17 cwt
	Tender	49 tons
Boiler Pressure:		280 lb/sq in (superheated)
Driving Wheels:		6 ft 3 in
Tractive Effort:		32,580 lb
Cylinders:		18½ in x 30 in
Piston valves.		

1000	*County of Middlesex*		1015	*County of Gloucester*
1001	*County of Bucks*		1016	*County of Hants*
1002	*County of Berks*		1017	*County of Hereford*
1003	*County of Wilts*		1018	*County of Leicester*
1004	*County of Somerset*		1019	*County of Merioneth*
1005	*County of Devon*		1020	*County of Monmouth*
1006	*County of Cornwall*		1021	*County of Montgomery*
1007	*County of Brecknock*		1022	*County of Northampton*
1008	*County of Cardigan*		1023	*County of Oxford*
1009	*County of Carmarthen*		1024	*County of Pembroke*
1010	*County of Caernarvon*		1025	*County of Radnor*
1011	*County of Chester*		1026	*County of Salop*
1012	*County of Denbigh*		1027	*County of Stafford*
1013	*County of Dorset*		1028	*County of Warwick*
1014	*County of Glamorgan*		1029	*County of Worcester*

The first example was built with a double blast pipe and chimney, others receiving them in later years. One member of the class, no. 1002, was allocated to Penzance depot and was often seen heading the final section of the prestigious 'The Cornish Riviera'. Unfortunately, none has survived into preservation.

The first member of the class, no. 1000 *County of Middlesex*, was built with a double blastpipe and chimney. The engine is seen here lying at the side of Reading depot under repair. Its pistons have been removed, presumably having failed in the area as it was allocated to Bristol Bath Road at this time.

7.8.55

Penzance depot's sole example of the 'County' class in the mid-fifties, no. 1002 *County of Berks*, has just worked in with 'The Cornish Riviera' and is still carrying the headboard.

7.8.55

4000 'Star' class 4–6–0 5P

The Stars were designed by Churchward for express passenger services; the original locomotive was in fact rebuilt from a 4–4–2 built in 1906.
Designer: G.J. Churchward.
Total built: 73.

Principal dimensions

Weight:	Locomotive	75 tons 12 cwt
	Tender	46 tons 14 cwt
Boiler Pressure:		225 lb/sq in (superheated)
Driving Wheels:		6 ft 8½ in
Tractive Effort:		27,800 lb
Cylinders:		(4) 15 in x 26 in

Inside Walschaerts valve gear and rocking levers for outside valves. Piston valves.

4056   *Princess Margaret*   4061   *Glastonbury Abbey*   4062   *Malmesbury Abbey*

By 1955 the 'Star' class was down to three examples, nos. 4056, 4061/2. There were originally seventy-three locomotives in the class, numbered 4000–72, and all were named, with successive batches named after stars, knights, kings (later to become monarchs), queens, princes, princesses and finally abbeys. Despite this mixture of names the class was generally known as the 'Stars'. Withdrawals commenced in the early thirties, the last survivor, no. 4056, remaining in service until 1957. One example of the class, no. 4003 *Lode Star*, built in 1907, is part of the National Collection at York Railway Museum.

'Star' class no. 4061 *Glastonbury Abbey* at Oxford coaling plant. This was a Wolverhampton Stafford Road engine and was withdrawn in 1957.

29.4.56

4073 'Castle' class 4–6–0 7P

Designer: C.B. Collett.
Total built: 168.

Principal dimensions

Weight:	Locomotive	79 tons 17 cwt
	Tender	46 tons 14 cwt
Boiler Pressure:		225 lb/sq in (superheated)
Driving Wheels:		6 ft 8½ in
Tractive Effort:		31,625 lb
Cylinders:		(4) 16 in x 26 in

Walschaerts valve gear – piston valves and rocking shafts.

4000	*North Star*	5006	*Treganna Castle*
4037	*The South Wales Borderers*	5007	*Rougemont Castle*
4073	*Caerphilly Castle*	5008	*Raglan Castle*
4074	*Caldicot Castle*	5009	*Shrewsbury Castle*
4075	*Cardiff Castle*	5010	*Restormel Castle*
4076	*Carmarthen Castle*	5011	*Tintagel Castle*
4077	*Chepstow Castle*	5012	*Berry Pomeroy Castle*
4078	*Pembroke Castle*	5013	*Abergavenny Castle*
4079	*Pendennis Castle*	5014	*Goodrich Castle*
4080	*Powderham Castle*	5015	*Kingswear Castle*
4081	*Warwick Castle*	5016	*Montgomery Castle*
4082	*Windsor Castle*	5017	*St. Donats Castle*
4083	*Abbotsbury Castle*	5018	*St. Mawes Castle*
4084	*Aberystwyth Castle*	5019	*Treago Castle*
4085	*Berkeley Castle*	5020	*Trematon Castle*
4086	*Builth Castle*	5021	*Whittington Castle*
4087	*Cardigan Castle*	5022	*Wigmore Castle*
4088	*Dartmouth Castle*	5023	*Brecon Castle*
4089	*Donnington Castle*	5024	*Carew Castle*
4090	*Dorchester Castle*	5025	*Chirk Castle*
4091	*Dudley Castle*	5026	*Criccieth Castle*
4092	*Dunraven Castle*	5027	*Farleigh Castle*
4093	*Dunster Castle*	5028	*Llantilio Castle*
4094	*Dybnevor Castle*	5029	*Nunney Castle*
4095	*Harlech Castle*	5030	*Shirburn Castle*
4096	*Highclere Castle*	5031	*Totnes Castle*
4097	*Kenilworth Castle*	5032	*Usk Castle*
4098	*Kidwelly Castle*	5033	*Broughton Castle*
4099	*Kilgerran Castle*	5034	*Corfe Castle*
5000	*Launceston Castle*	5035	*Coity Castle*
5001	*Llandovery Castle*	5036	*Lyonshall Castle*
5002	*Ludlow Castle*	5037	*Monmouth Castle*
5003	*Lulworth Castle*	5038	*Morlais Castle*
5004	*Llanstephan Castle*	5039	*Rhuddlan Castle*
5005	*Manorbier Castle*	5040	*Stokesay Castle*

5041	Tiverton Castle	5090	Neath Abbey
5042	Winchester Castle	5091	Cleeve Abbey
5043	Earl of Mount Edgcumbe	5092	Treso Abbey
5044	Earl of Dunraven	5093	Upton Castle
5045	Earl of Dudley	5094	Tretower Castle
5046	Earl Cawdor	5095	Barbury Castle
5047	Earl of Dartmouth	5096	Bridgwater Castle
5048	Earl of Devon	5097	Sarum Castle
5049	Earl of Plymouth	5098	Clifford Castle
5050	Earl of St. Germans	5099	Compton Castle
5051	Earl Bathurst	7000	Viscount Portal
5052	Earl of Radnor	7001	Sir James Milne
5053	Earl Cairns	7002	Devizes Castle
5054	Earl Ducie	7003	Elmley Castle
5055	Earl of Eldon	7004	Eastnor Castle
5056	Earl of Powis	7005	Lamphey Castle
5057	Earl Waldegrave	7006	Lydford Castle
5058	Earl of Clancarty	7007	Great Western
5059	Earl St. Aldwyn	7008	Swansea Castle
5060	Earl of Berkeley	7009	Athelney Castle
5061	Earl of Birkenhead	7010	Avondale Castle
5062	Earl of Shaftesbury	7011	Banbury Castle
5063	Earl Baldwin	7012	Barry Castle
5064	Bishop's Castle	7013	Bristol Castle
5065	Newport Castle	7014	Caerhays Castle
5066	Wardour Castle	7015	Carn Brea Castle
5067	St. Fagans Castle	7016	Chester Castle
5068	Beverston Castle	7017	G.J.Churchward
5069	Isambard Kingdom Brunel	7018	Drysllwyn Castle
5070	Sir Daniel Gooch	7019	Fowey Castle
5071	Spitfire	7020	Gloucester Castle
5072	Hurricane	7021	Haverfordwest Castle
5073	Blenheim	7022	Hereford Castle
5074	Hampden	7023	Penrice Castle
5075	Wellington	7024	Powis Castle
5076	Gladiator	7025	Sudeley Castle
5077	Fairey Battle	7026	Tenby Castle
5078	Beaufort	7027	Thornbury Castle
5079	Lysander	7028	Cadbury Castle
5080	Defiant	7029	Clun Castle
5081	Lockheed Hudson	7030	Cranbrook Castle
5082	Swordfish	7031	Cromwell's Castle
5083	Bath Abbey	7032	Denbigh Castle
5084	Reading Abbey	7033	Hartlebury Castle
5085	Evesham Abbey	7034	Ince Castle
5086	Viscount Horne	7035	Ogmore Castle
5087	Tintern Abbey	7036	Taunton Castle
5088	Llanthony Abbey	7037	Swindon
5089	Westminster Abbey		

In 1923 the first of the 'Castles' made its debut to a design by Collett. These powerful locomotives were developed from the 'Star' class and had a long history, with the last examples being built in British Railways days, the final one being completed in 1950. One of these is the well known no. 7029 *Clun Castle*.

These locomotives shared many of the principal express duties on the Western Region with the 'Kings'. Several 'Castles' were rebuilt from 'Stars' and one, no. 111 *Viscount Churchill*, withdrawn in 1953, was rebuilt from a 4–6–2. The next of the class to be withdrawn was no. 4000 *North Star* in 1957.

The 167 'Castles' in service during 1955 were to be found allocated to most of the principal Western Region depots with over thirty at Old Oak Common alone. Many were fitted with double chimneys.

Eight 'Castles' have survived: no. 4073 *Caerphilly Castle* at the Science Museum, no. 4079 *Pendennis Castle* in Australia and six others at preserved railways. The latter group are all engines built between 1924 and 1950.

'Castle' no. 5015 *Kingswear Castle* photographed at Oxford. Locomotives of the class were frequent visitors and the depot also had three in its own allocation during the mid-fifties.

27.3.55

Old Oak Common had over thirty members of the 'Castle' class including no. 7001 *Sir James Milne*, one of the later batch. Note the straight sided tender.

7.8.55

Newton Abbot 'Castle' no. 5071 *Spitfire*, still carrying 'The Cornishman' headboard, in the process of being serviced at Bristol Bath Road depot. This locomotive is running with a straight sided tender.

31.8.55

No. 5004 *Llanstephan Castle* was one of the large batch allocated to Old Oak Common. These powerful four cylinder locomotives were to be seen on most of the principal express trains.

7.8.55

No. 5045 *Earl of Dudley* drifts into Paddington at the end of the morning run from Worcester. The locomotive was showing signs of hard work on the smokebox door.

9.9.59

No. 7027 *Thornbury Castle*, built at Swindon in 1949, is one of the eight members of this class to survive. The locomotive is seen here at Oxford depot.

9.63

This freshly cleaned example of the 'Castle' class, no. 4037 *The South Wales Borderers*, was originally a member of the 'Star' class. In the mid-fifties it was a Penzance engine having for a number of years been at Old Oak Common.

6.9.56

This 'Castle' class locomotive no. 7030 *Cranbrook Castle* was only thirteen years old when this picture was taken at Oxford. The engine was withdrawn minus all plates and awaiting its final journey. The double chimney fitted to some members of the class can be clearly seen in this picture.

9.63

No. 7029 *Clun Castle* was built at Swindon in 1950 and worked many special trains in its final months of service. The locomotive is seen here at Banbury shed minus name, front and side number plates. *Clun Castle* has become one of the best known of all preserved locomotives and has worked many specials and been seen at many railway centres.

25.9.66

4900 'Hall' class 4–6–0 5MT

Designer: C.B. Collett.
Total built: 258.

Principal dimensions

Weight:	Locomotive	75 tons
	Tender	46 tons 14 cwt
Boiler Pressure:		225 lb/sq in (superheated)
Driving Wheels:		6 ft
Tractive Effort:		27,275 lb
Cylinders:		(0) 18½ in x 30 in

Stephenson valve gear.

The weight of the prototype, no. 4900, was 72 tons 10 cwt.

4900	*Saint Martin*		4932	*Hatherton Hall*
4901	*Adderley Hall*		4933	*Himley Hall*
4902	*Aldenham Hall*		4934	*Hindlip Hall*
4903	*Astley Hall*		4935	*Ketley Hall*
4904	*Binnegar Hall*		4936	*Kinlet Hall*
4905	*Barton Hall*		4937	*Lanelay Hall*
4906	*Bradfield Hall*		4938	*Liddington Hall*
4907	*Broughton Hall*		4939	*Littleton Hall*
4908	*Broome Hall*		4940	*Ludford Hall*
4909	*Blakesley Hall*		4941	*Llangedwyn Hall*
4910	*Blaisdon Hall*		4942	*Maindy Hall*
4912	*Berrington Hall*		4943	*Marrington Hall*
4913	*Baglan Hall*		4944	*Middleton Hall*
4914	*Cranmore Hall*		4945	*Milligan Hall*
4915	*Condover Hall*		4946	*Moseley Hall*
4916	*Crumlin Hall*		4947	*Nanhoran Hall*
4917	*Crosswood Hall*		4948	*Northwick Hall*
4918	*Dartington Hall*		4949	*Packwood Hall*
4919	*Donnington Hall*		4950	*Patshull Hall*
4920	*Dumbleton Hall*		4951	*Pendeford Hall*
4921	*Eaton Hall*		4952	*Peplow Hall*
4922	*Enville Hall*		4953	*Pitchford Hall*
4923	*Evenley Hall*		4954	*Plaish Hall*
4924	*Eydon Hall*		4955	*Plaspower Hall*
4925	*Eynsham Hall*		4956	*Plowden Hall*
4926	*Fairleigh Hall*		4957	*Postlip Hall*
4827	*Farnborough Hall*		4958	*Priory Hall*
4928	*Gatacre Hall*		4959	*Purley Hall*
4929	*Goytrey Hall*		4960	*Pyle Hall*
4930	*Hagley Hall*		4961	*Pyrland Hall*
4931	*Hanbury Hall*		4962	*Ragley Hall*

4963	Rignall Hall	5912	Queen's Hall
4964	Rodwell Hall	5913	Rushton Hall
4965	Rood Ashton Hall	5914	Ripon Hall
4966	Shakenhurst Hall	5915	Trentham Hall
4967	Shirenewton Hall	5916	Trinity Hall
4968	Shotton Hall	5917	Westminster Hall
4969	Shrugborough Hall	5918	Walton Hall
4970	Sketty Hall	5919	Worsley Hall
4971	Stanway Hall	5920	Wycliffe Hall
4972	Saint Brides Hall	5921	Bingley Hall
4973	Sweeney Hall	5922	Caxton Hall
4974	Talgarth Hall	5923	Colston Hall
4975	Umberslade Hall	5924	Dinton Hall
4976	Warfield Hall	5925	Eastcote Hall
4977	Watcombe Hall	5926	Grotrian Hall
4978	Westwood Hall	5927	Guild Hall
4979	Wootton Hall	5928	Haddon Hall
4980	Wrottesley Hall	5929	Hanham Hall
4981	Abberley Hall	5930	Hannington Hall
4982	Acton Hall	5931	Hatherley Hall
4983	Albert Hall	5932	Haydon Hall
4984	Albrighton Hall	5933	Kingsway Hall
4985	Allesley Hall	5934	Kneller Hall
4986	Aston Hall	5935	Norton Hall
4987	Brockley Hall	5936	Oakley Hall
4988	Bulwell Hall	5937	Stanford Hall
4989	Cherwell Hall	5938	Stanley Hall
4990	Clifton Hall	5939	Tangley Hall
4991	Cobham Hall	5940	Whitbourne Hall
4992	Crosby Hall	5941	Campion Hall
4993	Dalton Hall	5942	Doldowlod Hall
4994	Downton Hall	5943	Elmdon Hall
4995	Easton Hall	5944	Ickenham Hall
4996	Eden Hall	5945	Leckhampton Hall
4997	Elton Hall	5946	Marwell Hall
4998	Eyton Hall	5947	Saint Benet's Hall
4999	Gopsal Hall	5948	Siddington Hall
5900	Hinderton Hall	5949	Trematon Hall
5901	Hazel Hall	5950	Wardley Hall
5902	Howick Hall	5951	Clyffe Hall
5903	Keele Hall	5952	Cogan Hall
5904	Kelham Hall	5953	Dunley Hall
5905	Knowsley Hall	5954	Faendre Hall
5906	Lawton Hall	5955	Garth Hall
5907	Marble Hall	5956	Horsley Hall
5908	Moreton Hall	5957	Hutton Hall
5909	Newton Hall	5958	Knolton Hall
5910	Park Hall	5959	Mawley Hall
5911	Preston Hall	5960	Saint Edmund Hall

5961	Toynbee Hall	6910	Gossington Hall
5962	Wantage Hall	6911	Holker Hall
5963	Wimpole Hall	6912	Helmster Hall
5964	Wolseley Hall	6913	Levens Hall
5965	Woollas Hall	6914	Langton Hall
5966	Ashford Hall	6915	Mursley Hall
5967	Bickmarsh Hall	6916	Misterton Hall
5968	Cory Hall	6917	Oldlands Hall
5969	Honington Hall	6918	Sandon Hall
5970	Hengrave Hall	6919	Tylney Hall
5971	Merevale Hall	6920	Barningham Hall
5972	Olton Hall	6921	Borwick Hall
5973	Rolleston Hall	6922	Burton Hall
5974	Wallsworth Hall	6923	Croxteth Hall
5975	Winslow Hall	6924	Grantley Hall
5976	Ashwicke Hall	6925	Hackness Hall
5977	Beckford Hall	6926	Holkham Hall
5978	Bodinnick Hall	6927	Lilford Hall
5979	Cruckton Hall	6928	Underley Hall
5980	Dingley Hall	6929	Whorlton Hall
5981	Frensham Hall	6930	Aldersey Hall
5982	Harrington Hall	6931	Aldborough Hall
5983	Henley Hall	6932	Burwarton Hall
5984	Linden Hall	6933	Birtles Hall
5985	Mostyn Hall	6934	Beachamwell Hall
5986	Arbury Hall	6935	Browsholme Hall
5987	Brocket Hall	6936	Breccles Hall
5988	Bostock Hall	6937	Conyngham Hall
5989	Cransley Hall	6938	Corndean Hall
5990	Dorford Hall	6939	Calveley Hall
5991	Gresham Hall	6940	Didlington Hall
5992	Horton Hall	6941	Fillongley Hall
5993	Kirby Hall	6942	Eshton Hall
5994	Roydon Hall	6943	Farnley Hall
5995	Wick Hall	6944	Fledborough Hall
5996	Mytton Hall	6945	Glasfryn Hall
5997	Sparkford Hall	6946	Heatherden Hall
5998	Trevor Hall	6947	Helmingham Hall
5999	Wollaton Hall	6948	Holbrooke Hall
6900	Abney Hall	6949	Haberfield Hall
6901	Arley Hall	6950	Kingsthorpe Hall
6902	Butlers Hall	6951	Impney Hall
6903	Belmont Hall	6952	Kimberley Hall
6904	Charfield Hall	6953	Leighton Hall
6905	Claughton Hall	6954	Lotherton Hall
6906	Chicheley Hall	6955	Lydcott Hall
6907	Davenham Hall	6956	Mottram Hall
6908	Downham Hall	6957	Norcliffe Hall
6909	Frewin Hall	6958	Oxburgh Hall

This was one of the most numerous of all Great Western classes, comprising 258 locomotives all named after Halls with one exception, no. 4900 *Saint Martin*. This was the first locomotive of the class and was rebuilt from a 'Saint' to a Collett design in 1924, the original locomotive dating from 1907. In 1928 the first of the new construction was completed. This had a higher pitched boiler, modified footplating and other detail differences. One locomotive, no. 4911, was destroyed during an air raid in the early part of the war. The prototype of the class, no. 4900, was withdrawn in 1959. Eleven examples have survived into preservation, due in no small part to many Western Region engines ending up in Barry scrapyard.

The prototype of the 'Hall' class, no. 4900 *Saint Martin*, was allocated to Newton Abbot depot in the mid-fifties and is seen here at Plymouth Laira shed. This engine was rebuilt from a 'Saint' class in 1924 to a Collett design. The new construction differed slightly in that the boiler was pitched higher and there were also other detail differences.

4.9.56

Quite a sizeable batch of 'Halls' were to be found at Cardiff Canton depot. No. 4968 *Shotton Hall* was one of them. The locomotive is seen here at Cardiff General station heading a Bristol train.

30.8.55

'Halls' were to be found at the great majority of the Western Region depots. No. 4936 *Kinlet Hall* is seen here at Exeter, its home depot. This locomotive is one of the lucky survivors and is to be seen at the Llangollen Railway.

4.9.56

The 'Halls' were popular and powerful locomotives equally at home on passenger or freight workings. No. 6925 *Hackness Hall* is seen here at Oxford depot slowly producing a large puddle in the shed yard.

29.4.56

Members of the 'Hall' class were commonplace at Oxford, not just the depot's own locomotives but the many visitors which worked in daily. No. 6910 *Gossington Hall* was a Didcot engine and is shown here about to pick up its return working.

29.4.56

'Hall' class no. 5992 *Horton Hall* pictured at Bristol Bath Road. This shed had over ninety engines in its allocation during the mid-fifties, including a sizeable number of 'Halls'.

31.8.55

By 1956 no. 4948 *Northwick Hall* had moved from Cardiff Canton and was allocated to Exeter. The engine is seen here at Plymouth Laira depot. Locomotive movements such as this were fairly commonplace in the fifties.

4.9.56

6000 'King' class 4–6–0 8P

Designer: C.B. Collett.
Total built: 30.

Principal dimensions

Weight:	Locomotive	89 tons
	Tender	46 tons 14 cwt
Boiler Pressure:		250 lb/sq in (superheated)
Driving Wheels:		6 ft 6 in
Tractive Effort:		40,285 lb
Cylinders:		(4) 18½ in x 30 in

Walschaert valve gear.

6000	*King George V*		6015	*King Richard III*
6001	*King Edward VII*		6016	*King Edward V*
6002	*King William IV*		6017	*King Edward IV*
6003	*King George IV*		6018	*King Henry VI*
6004	*King George III*		6019	*King Henry V*
6005	*King George II*		6020	*King Henry IV*
6006	*King George I*		6021	*King Richard II*
6007	*King William III*		6022	*King Edward III*
6008	*King James II*		6023	*King Edward II*
6009	*King Charles II*		6024	*King Edward I*
6010	*King Charles I*		6025	*King Henry III*
6011	*King James I*		6026	*King John*
6012	*King Edward VI*		6027	*King Richard I*
6013	*King Henry VIII*		6028	*King George VI*
6014	*King Henry VII*		6029	*King Edward VIII*

The class was introduced in 1927 to a design by Collett, construction being over a three year period. In their later years they were fitted with double blastpipes and chimneys. These were the principal express passenger locomotives of the Great Western and later Western Region and as such were to be found on 'The Cornish Riviera' and other important express services. Three examples of the class have survived: no. 6000 *King George V*, part of the National Collection and to be found at the Great Western Museum, and nos. 6023/4 *King Edward II* and *King Edward I* respectively, both built in 1930.

'King' class no. 6008 *King James II* backs out of Paddington station after being released by one of the station pilots. The engine had been fitted with double blastpipe and chimney as were all the class in their later years.

9.9.59

Old Oak Common 'King' no. 6009 *King Charles II* at Bristol Bath Road depot. The engine was in steam when this picture was taken. Note the safety valve cover is missing but whether this had been lost en route or taken off on arrival is not known.

31.8.55

Twelve examples of the 'King' class were allocated to Old Oak Common in the mid-fifties, including the one seen here, no. 6012 *King Edward VI*, which had previously been at Plymouth Laira.

7.8.55

Taking water at its home shed at Old Oak Common is no. 6009 *King Charles II*. The thirty-strong 'King' class was allocated to just three depots: Old Oak Common, Plymouth Laira and Wolverhampton Stafford Road.

7.8.55

6800 'Grange' class 4–6–0 5MT

Designer: C.B. Collett.
Total built: 80, 1936–9, all named.

Principal dimensions

Weight:	Locomotive	74 tons
	Tender	40 tons

Boiler Pressure:	225 lb/sq in (superheated)
Driving Wheels:	5 ft 8 in
Tractive Effort:	28,875 lb
Cylinders:	(O) 18½ in x 30 in

Piston valves.

6800	*Arlington Grange*		6834	*Dummer Grange*
6801	*Aylburton Grange*		6835	*Eastham Grange*
6802	*Bampton Grange*		6836	*Estevarney Grange*
6803	*Bucklebury Grange*		6837	*Forthampton Grange*
6804	*Brockington Grange*		6838	*Goodmoor Grange*
6805	*Broughton Grange*		6839	*Hewell Grange*
6806	*Blackwell Grange*		6840	*Hazeley Grange*
6807	*Birchwood Grange*		6841	*Marlas Grange*
6808	*Beenham Grange*		6842	*Nunhold Grange*
6809	*Burghclere Grange*		6843	*Poulton Grange*
6810	*Blakemere Grange*		6844	*Penhydd Grange*
6811	*Cranbourne Grange*		6845	*Paviland Grange*
6812	*Chesford Grange*		6846	*Ruckley Grange*
6813	*Eastbury Grange*		6847	*Tidmarsh Grange*
6814	*Enborne Grange*		6848	*Toddington Grange*
6815	*Frilford Grange*		6849	*Walton Grange*
6816	*Frankton Grange*		6850	*Cleeve Grange*
6817	*Gwenddwr Grange*		6851	*Hurst Grange*
6818	*Hardwick Grange*		6852	*Headbourne Grange*
6819	*Highnam Grange*		6853	*Morehampton Grange*
6820	*Kingstone Grange*		6854	*Roundhill Grange*
6821	*Leaton Grange*		6855	*Saighton Grange*
6822	*Manton Grange*		6856	*Stowe Grange*
6823	*Oakley Grange*		6857	*Tudor Grange*
6824	*Ashley Grange*		6858	*Woolston Grange*
6825	*Llanvair Grange*		6859	*Yiewsley Grange*
6826	*Nannerth Grange*		6860	*Aberporth Grange*
6827	*Llanfrechfa Grange*		6861	*Crynant Grange*
6828	*Trellech Grange*		6862	*Derwent Grange*
6829	*Burmington Grange*		6863	*Dolhywel Grange*
6830	*Buckenhill Grange*		6864	*Dymock Grange*
6831	*Bearley Grange*		6865	*Hopton Grange*
6832	*Brockton Grange*		6866	*Morfa Grange*
6833	*Calcot Grange*		6867	*Peterston Grange*

6868	Penrhos Grange	6874	Haughton Grange
6869	Resolven Grange	6875	Hindford Grange
6870	Bodicote Grange	6876	Kingsland Grange
6871	Bourton Grange	6877	Llanfair Grange
6872	Crawley Grange	6878	Longford Grange
6873	Caradoc Grange	6879	Overton Grange

These engines were basically a variation of the 'Halls'. They were fitted with 5 ft 8 in wheels as opposed to the 6 ft of the 'Halls' and some parts from withdrawn 4300 class Moguls were incorporated. The 'Granges' were designed by Collett and made their debut on the Great Western in 1936. They were designed as mixed traffic engines although they were often to be seen on passenger services, especially in the West Country. Unfortunately, all the class was cut up, many at private scrapyards.

Although designed for mixed traffic the 'Granges' were often seen on passenger workings. No. 6824 *Ashley Grange* was photographed at Truro heading a local passenger for Penzance. This locomotive was one of twelve engines of the class allocated to Penzance depot (83G) at this time.

6.9.56

Examples of the eighty-strong 'Grange' class were to be found at many Western Region depots. No. 6874 *Haughton Grange* was photographed at Banbury having worked in from Didcot.

9.63

Quite a considerable number of the 'Grange' class were allocated to depots in the West Country. No. 6802 *Bampton Grange*, seen here at Newton Abbot awaiting its return working to Plymouth Laira, was one of seven allocated at this time.

4.9.56

No. 6863 *Dolhywel Grange* seen here in the spacious roundhouse at Bristol St Phillips Marsh depot. Note the locomotive boiler in the background in use as a stationary boiler at this time. St Phillips Marsh had a considerable number of 'Granges' in its allocation.

31.8.55

6959 'Modified Hall' class 4–6–0 5MT

Designer: F.W. Hawksworth.
Total built: 71, 1944–50.

Principal dimensions

Weight:	Locomotive	75 tons 16 cwt
	Tender	46 tons 14 cwt
Boiler Pressure:		225 lb/sq in (superheated)
Driving Wheels:		6 ft
Tractive Effort:		27,275 lb
Cylinders:		(O) 18½ in x 30 in

Stephenson valve gear – piston valves.

6959	*Peatling Hall*		6995	*Benthall Hall*
6960	*Raveningham Hall*		6996	*Blackwell Hall*
6961	*Stedham Hall*		6997	*Bryn-Ivor Hall*
6962	*Soughton Hall*		6998	*Burton Agnes Hall*
6963	*Throwley Hall*		6999	*Capel Dewi Hall*
6964	*Thornbridge Hall*		7900	*St. Peter's Hall*
6965	*Thirlestaine Hall*		7901	*Dodington Hall*
6966	*Witchingham Hall*		7902	*Eaton Mascot Hall*
6967	*Willesley Hall*		7903	*Foremarke Hall*
6968	*Woodcock Hall*		7904	*Fountains Hall*
6969	*Wraysbury Hall*		7905	*Fowey Hall*
6970	*Whaddon Hall*		7906	*Fron Hall*
6971	*Athelhampton Hall*		7907	*Hart Hall*
6972	*Beningborough Hall*		7908	*Henshall Hall*
6973	*Bricklehampton Hall*		7909	*Heveningham Hall*
6974	*Bryngwyn Hall*		7910	*Hown Hall*
6975	*Capesthorne Hall*		7911	*Lady Margaret Hall*
6976	*Graythwaite Hall*		7912	*Little Linford Hall*
6977	*Grundisburgh Hall*		7913	*Little Wyrley Hall*
6978	*Haroldstone Hall*		7914	*Lleweni Hall*
6979	*Helperly Hall*		7915	*Mere Hall*
6980	*Llanrumney Hall*		7916	*Mobberley Hall*
6981	*Marbury Hall*		7917	*North Aston Hall*
6982	*Melmerby Hall*		7918	*Rhose Wood Hall*
6983	*Otterington Hall*		7919	*Runter Hall*
6984	*Owsden Hall*		7920	*Coney Hall*
6985	*Parwick Hall*		7921	*Edstone Hall*
6986	*Rydal Hall*		7922	*Salford Hall*
6987	*Shervington Hall*		7923	*Speke Hall*
6988	*Swithland Hall*		7924	*Thornycroft Hall*
6989	*Wightwick Hall*		7925	*Westol Hall*
6990	*Witherslack Hall*		7926	*Willey Hall*
6991	*Acton Burnell Hall*		7927	*Willington Hall*
6992	*Arborfield Hall*		7928	*Wolf Hall*
6993	*Arthog Hall*		7929	*Wyke Hall*
6994	*Baggrave Hall*			

These were a development of the 'Hall' class introduced by Hawksworth in 1944, with a total of seventy-one locomotives built over the period 1944–50. They were fitted with larger superheaters, one piece main frames and a plate framed bogie. These engines were in two number series 6959–99 and 7900–29 and all were named. Seven locomotives have survived into preservation.

Having been released from its train by one of Paddington's station pilots, 'Modified Hall' no. 7921 *Edstone Hall* backs out for servicing. This engine was allocated to Chester depot at this time.

7.8.55

'Modified Hall' no. 7911 *Lady Margaret Hall* photographed outside its home depot, Oxford. Note the large accumulation of coal dust, ash, etc. that completely hides the sleepers.

9.63

Several examples of the 'Modified Hall' class could usually be found at Banbury shed. No. 6979 *Helperly Hall* was ready for an express train duty when this picture was taken.

9.63

No. 6994 *Baggrave Hall* had recently received the attention of cleaners and was shining in the evening light as it was shunted at Banbury depot. This was an Oswestry engine and was fitted with a straight sided tender at this time.

9.63

7800 'Manor' class 4–6–0 5MT

Designer: C.B. Collett.
Total built: 30, all named.

Principal dimensions

Weight:	Locomotive	68 tons 18 cwt
	Tender	40 tons
Boiler Pressure:		225 lb/sq in (superheated)
Driving Wheels:		5 ft 8 in
Tractive Effort:		27,340 lb
Cylinders:		(0) 18 in x 30 in

Stephenson valve gear – piston valves.

7800	*Torquay Manor*	7815	*Fritwell Manor*
7801	*Anthony Manor*	7816	*Frilsham Manor*
7802	*Bradley Manor*	7817	*Garsington Manor*
7803	*Barcote Manor*	7818	*Granville Manor*
7804	*Baydon Manor*	7819	*Hinton Manor*
7805	*Broome Manor*	7820	*Dinmore Manor*
7806	*Cockington Manor*	7821	*Ditcheat Manor*
7807	*Compton Manor*	7822	*Foxcote Manor*
7808	*Cookham Manor*	7823	*Hook Norton Manor*
7809	*Childrey Manor*	7824	*Iford Manor*
7810	*Draycott Manor*	7825	*Lechlade Manor*
7811	*Dunley Manor*	7826	*Longworth Manor*
7812	*Erlestoke Manor*	7827	*Lydham Manor*
7813	*Freshford Manor*	7828	*Odney Manor*
7814	*Fringford Manor*	7829	*Ramsbury Manor*

These engines were designed principally for use on secondary and cross country lines where weight restrictions prevented larger engines such as 'Halls' and 'Granges' being used. The 'Manors' were extensively used on the Cambrian and in the West Country. They were first introduced in 1938, twenty being built in 1938/9, and a further ten were built after nationalization in 1950. It was originally intended to construct one hundred engines of this Collett design. Fortunately, nine have survived into preservation, five of which are from the 1950 batch.

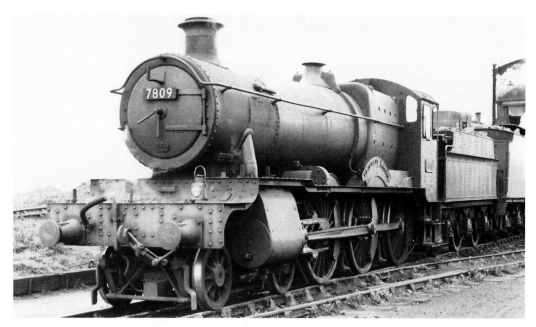

My first picture of no. 7809 *Childrey Manor* was taken at Plymouth Laira depot where it was allocated with four other members of the class in the mid-fifties. This engine was one of the first batch to be constructed.

4.9.56

No. 7809 *Childrey Manor* again, this time at Aberystwyth. The engine was now working on the Cambrian line in company with several other classmates. In the background is Standard Class 2 no. 78003. These 2MTs worked most of the freight traffic in the area having taken over most of the duties once worked by 2251 class 0–6–0s and Moguls.

7.61

Withdrawn locomotives were to be found at many Western Region depots during 1965 awaiting their final journey. No. 7814 *Fringford Manor* is seen here at Gloucester with name, cabside and front number plates all removed. Locomotives were usually towed in batches to scrapyards.

27.10.65

9000 class 4–4–0 2P

Designer: C.B. Collett (rebuild).
Total built: 30.

Principal dimensions

Weight:	Locomotive	49 tons
	Tender	40 tons
Boiler Pressure:		180 lb/sq in
Driving Wheels:		5 ft 8 in
Tractive Effort:		18,955 lb
Cylinders:		18 in x 26 in

Stephenson valve gear.

The only 4–4–0 design in regular service on the Western Region was the 9000 class commonly known as 'Dukedogs'. Introduced in 1936, these outside framed locomotives on first appearance looked much older. They were Collett rebuilds incorporating boilers from withdrawn 'Duke of Cornwall' class and 'Bulldog' class frames. Thirty were built numbered 3200–28 over a three year period. In 1946 they were renumbered 9000–29. The first twelve engines were named after Earls but this was short lived, the names being removed and transferred to Castles. Withdrawals commenced in 1948 but one still survives, no. 9017 built in 1938.

One 'Dukedog' was allocated to Oxford. On my visits in the mid-fifties the engine was present on each occasion usually not in steam. On a cold frosty morning no. 9015 was being shunted by a 'Castle' class. These engines with their outside frames presented an unusual appearance against the modern Great Western designs.

27.2.55

'Dukedog' no. 9015 again at Oxford. Judging by the coal in the tender it had only just been filled. Note the large lumps. These engines incorporated boilers from withdrawn 'Duke' class engines and frames from 'Bulldogs'.

31.10.54

2800 class 2–8–0 8F

Designer: G.J. Churchward/C.B. Collett.
Total built: 167.

Principal dimensions

Weight:	Locomotive	75–76 tons
	Tender	40 tons
Boiler Pressure:		225 lb/sq in (superheated)
Driving Wheels:		4 ft 7½ in
Tractive Effort:		35,380 lb
Cylinders:		(0) 18½ in x 30 in

Stephenson valve gear.

These were the Great Western heavy freight locomotives. The design was first introduced by Churchward in 1903, construction lasting until 1919. In 1938 a further batch was built under the design of Collett, these locomotives having side window cabs and other slight modifications, greatly improving the conditions for enginemen. The later engines were sometimes referred to as the 2884 class. Withdrawals commenced in 1958 and in two years no less than forty had made their final journey. Sixteen have survived, one, no. 2818, being part of the National Collection.

Bristol St Phillips Marsh was home for a number of the 2800 class. No. 2875 was among the last of the first batch to be constructed. These sturdy 2–8–0s had a tractive effort higher than the London Midland Region 8Fs.

31.8.55

Rather surprisingly Plymouth Laira had only two members of the class in its allocation during the mid-fifties. No. 2843 was the oldest of the pair and when photographed it was lying at the back of the shed.

4.9.56

2800 class no. 3841, a side window cab engine, had recently received the attention of cleaners, a rare event for goods engines in the mid-fifties. The locomotive is seen here at the back of Bristol St Phillips Marsh depot.

31.8.55

Old Oak Common had a repair shop adjacent to the shed. No. 3853 is seen outside receiving attention to a pair of driving wheels. This engine was one of the 2800 class allocated to this depot.

9.9.51

By 1963 many Western Region locomotives had lost various plates but no. 2890 at Oxford depot still had its complete set. This engine was one of the batch introduced in 1938, fitted with a side window cab and having various detail alterations.

9.63

4700 class 2–8–0 7F

Designer: G.J. Churchward.
Total built: 9.

Principal dimensions

Weight:	Locomotive	82 tons
	Tender	46 tons 14 cwt
Boiler Pressure:		225 lb/sq in (superheated)
Driving Wheels:		5 ft 8 in
Tractive Effort:		30,460 lb
Cylinders:		(0) 19 in x 30 in
Piston valves.		

    These powerful locomotives were designed principally for fast goods workings, although they were often commandeered for passenger trains, particularly specials and excursions. Only nine were built to a Churchward design, first making their appearance in 1919. The majority of the class were allocated in the mid-fifties to Old Oak Common depot, the remaining two being at Bristol St Phillips Marsh. Unfortunately, all were cut up on withdrawal from service.

One of the 4700 class could often be found at Banbury having worked in from London overnight on a fast goods. No. 4701 is seen here awaiting its return working.

27.3.55

Another view of no. 4701 which illustrates clearly its 5 ft 8 in driving wheels as opposed to the 4 ft 7½ in of the 2800 class heavy freight 2–8–0s. Unfortunately no examples of this class have survived.

27.3.55

ROD class 2–8–0 7F

Designer: J.G. Robinson.

Principal dimensions

Weight:	Locomotive	73 tons 11 cwt
	Tender	47 tons 14 cwt
Boiler Pressure:		185 lb/sq in (superheated)
Driving Wheels:		4 ft 8 in
Tractive Effort:		32,200 lb
Cylinders:		(O) 21 in x 26 in

Piston valves.

The successful Robinson 2–8–0 heavy freight locomotive designed for the Great Central Railway was chosen for production of locomotives for the War Department and a large number were constructed. After the cessation of hostilities these engines became available and the Great Western was one of the railways to purchase some, buying up a hundred between 1919 and 1921. These were duly 'Westernized' with new chimney, dome, top feed, safety valve cover, etc. and, of course, cab side number plates. Despite all this the unmistakable outline of the Great Central design was easily recognizable. Their numbers had been greatly reduced by the mid-fifties and all were scrapped by the end of 1958.

45

The unmistakable outline of the Robinson Great Central design can be easily seen despite the Great Western fittings it had received over the years since purchased from the War Department after the end of the First World War.

31.10.54

4300 class 2–6–0 4MT

Designer: G.J. Churchward.
Total built: 342, 1911–32.

Principal dimensions

Weight:	Locomotive	62–65 tons
	Tender	40 tons
Boiler Pressure:		200 lb/sq in (superheated)
Driving Wheels:		5 ft 8 in
Tractive Effort:		25,670 lb
Cylinders:		(0) 18½ in x 30 in

Stephenson valve gear.

Every region had its 'Maids of all work'. Among those on the Western were the 2–6–0 Moguls first introduced in 1911 to a Churchward design and equally at home on passenger or goods work. These engines were built over a long period during which time there were various alterations. Twenty of those completed in 1932 had side window cabs. In 1956 the twenty engines with cabs became nos. 7322–41. Only two survive: one without side window cab, the other, no. 7325, on the Severn Valley Railway.

Mogul no. 6360, a Swindon engine, is seen here at Bedford, way off its home territory, after working in with a rugby special. Many of the Moguls were re-numbered during the late fifties.

23.2.52

Twenty Moguls were built with side window cabs, no. 9311 being one. The engine is seen here at Oxford depot shortly before re-numbering. Locomotives of Western, Southern, London Midland and Eastern Regions were often to be seen here at this time.

29.4.56

Five of the side window cab Moguls were to be found at Southall shed. No. 9305, seen here at Oxford, was one and this engine was later re-numbered to no. 7327. The Moguls were popular and very useful engines and were to be seen on passenger and goods work.

31.10.54

Mogul no. 6367 must have been lying at the siding of Banbury depot for some considerable time when this picture was taken as the sheeting used to cover the chimney had long since become loose. The Moguls were mixed traffic engines and were often seen on passenger work.

9.63

2251 class 0–6–0 3MT

Designer: C.B. Collett.
Total built: 120.

Principal dimensions

Weight:	Locomotive	43 tons 8 cwt
	Tender	36 tons 15 cwt
Boiler Pressure:		200 lb/sq in (superheated)
Driving Wheels:		5 ft 2 in
Tractive Effort:		20,155 lb
Cylinders:		$17\frac{1}{2}$ in x 24 in

Stephenson valve gear.

Tender locomotives of the 0–6–0 wheel arrangement were not very common on the Western Region from where the last remaining examples of the 'Dean Goods' were withdrawn in 1957, leaving only one design of this wheel arrangement, the 2251 class. They were built over a long period from 1930 with the last completed in 1948. They were a Collett design and used on a wide variety of duties. Only one, no. 3205, survives. This was for many years on the Severn Valley Railway but lately it has been at the West Somerset Railway.

No. 2201 awaits its turn alongside the typical Great Western coaling and water storage facility at Bristol St Phillips Marsh depot. Behind the locomotive's buffer beam discussion would appear to be taking place regarding the sets of fire irons stored there.

31.8.55

This immaculate example of the 2251 class, no. 2211, had recently received a general overhaul. The engine was allocated to Exeter depot (83C) where this picture was taken.

14.9.56

2301 class 0–6–0 2MT

Designer: W. Dean.
Total built: 280, 1883–99.

Principal dimensions

Weight:	Locomotive	36 tons 16 cwt
	Tender	34 tons 5 cwt
Boiler Pressure:		180 lb/sq in (superheated)
Driving Wheels:		5 ft 2 in
Tractive Effort:		18,140 lb
Cylinders:		17 in x 24 in

Stephenson valve gear.

At the beginning of 1955 only four examples of the famous 'Dean Goods' remained in service. Two of these were withdrawn during the year with the remaining two soldiering on until 1956 and 1957. This was one of the classic Great Western designs first introduced by Dean in 1883. Twenty of the locomotives were built with outside frames.

During the First World War locomotives were loaned to the War Department by most of the railway companies for service on the Continent. Among these were a considerable number of 'Dean Goods'. Fortunately, one member of the class, no. 2516, has been preserved as part of the National Collection at the Great Western Railway Museum, Swindon.

One of the last four 'Dean Goods' in service was no. 2513 seen here at Chester depot. This engine was withdrawn from service at Chester in 1955. Fortunately, one of these very important Great Western designs is preserved as part of the National Collection.

12.8.52

7200 class 2–8–2T 8F

Designer: C.B. Collett (rebuild of Churchward design).
Total built: 54.

Principal dimensions

Weight:	92 tons 2 cwt
Boiler Pressure:	200 lb/sq in (superheated)
Driving Wheels:	4 ft 7½ in
Tractive Effort:	33,170 lb
Cylinders:	(0) 19 in x 30 in

Stephenson valve gear.

The fifty-four members of this class were all rebuilds of 4200 and 5205 class 2–8–0Ts. Rebuilding commenced in 1934 to a design by Collett. This included a larger coal bunker considerably extending their range and the addition of a set of trailing wheels. Three of these massive tank engines are still with us today.

The 7200 class was the largest tank design to be found on the Western Region. These powerful locomotives weighed 92 tons. Here no. 7246 awaits servicing at Oxford depot. Four members of the class were allocated here.

29.4.56

The large coal bunker on the 7200 class can be clearly seen in this picture of no. 7207 at Oxford in company with Stanier 8F 2–8–0 no. 48011. It would appear that some modification had been made to the locomotive's cab.

9.63

4200 class 2–8–0T 7F

Designer: G.J. Churchward.

Principal dimensions

	4200	5205
Weight:	81 tons 12 cwt	82 tons 2 cwt
Boiler Pressure:	200 lb/sq in	200 lb/sq in
Driving Wheels:	4 ft 7½ in	4 ft 7½ in
Tractive Effort:	31,450 lb	33,170 lb
Cylinders:	18½ in x 30 in	19 in x 30 in

Stephenson valve gear.

These heavy freight engines were designed for short haul mineral trains and were often to be seen handling coal traffic from the South Wales pits. They were first introduced in 1910 to a Churchward design. In 1923 a variation known as the 5205 class appeared, having larger cylinders and other detail differences. As a result they were classified 8F. Fifty-four members of the class were rebuilt as 2–8–2Ts which became 7200 class. Three locomotives have survived.

No. 5264 was built in 1940 as the last of the class. The engine is one of the variations known as the 5205 class. It is seen here at Bristol St Phillips Marsh heading a heavy coal train.

31.8.55

The massive proportions of 5205 class no. 5208 can be clearly seen from this picture taken at Swindon Works yard. Many of these powerful locomotives were to be found in South Wales where they were frequently employed on handling coal traffic.

4.2.53

In 1965 the locomotives at Barry scrapyard looked very different after years of exposure to salt laden air. No. 4277 was virtually intact when this picture was taken, apart from the coupling rods; this engine was later rescued for preservation.

25.10.65

4500 class 2–6–2T 4MT

Designer: G.J. Churchward/C.B. Collett.
Total built: 175.

Principal dimensions

Weight:	57 tons (61 tons for 4575 class)
Boiler Pressure:	200 lb/sq in (superheated)
Driving Wheels:	4 ft 7½ in
Tractive Effort:	21,250 lb
Cylinders:	17 in x 24 in

Stephenson valve gear.

These very useful tank locomotives were designed for branch line and carriage pilot duties, being a development of the earlier 4400 class, the last of which was withdrawn in 1954. Introduced by Churchward in 1906 they were to be found at many depots in the West Country during the fifties. One example was St Blazey in Cornwall which had eleven in its allocation, just under a third of the depot's total number of locomotives.

In 1927 a slightly heavier version was introduced by Collett which had detail alterations such as larger tanks. As a result they were classified 4575 class.

They are ideal locomotives for use on preserved lines and fourteen have survived. Some of these spent years lying at Barry scrapyard from where they were rescued in an extremely derelict condition.

No. 4520 seen here at Swindon Works was one of the Churchward-designed locomotives first introduced in 1906.

4.2.53

Eleven of these 2–6–2Ts, a mixture of 4500 and 4575 classes, were allocated to St Blazey. No. 5519 is seen outside its home shed.

6.9.55

Early evening at Westbury and no. 5554, one of two 4575 class locomotives based at the depot, has returned after its day's work. Note the interesting vehicle in the background, part of the depot's breakdown train.

31.8.55

Bristol Bath Road shed had twenty-three of the 4500/4575 class in its allocation of ninety-one. Among these was no. 5561, built at Swindon in the late twenties. Weighing just 61 tons these engines were the lightest of the 2–6–2Ts in service on the ex-Great Western with the exception of the 'Vale of Rheidol' narrow gauge locomotives.

31.8.55

5100 class 2–6–2T 4MT

Designer: C.B. Collett.

Principal dimensions

Weight:	75 tons 10 cwt
Boiler Pressure:	200 lb/sq in (superheated)
Driving Wheels:	5 ft 8 in
Tractive Effort:	24,300 lb
Cylinders:	(0) 18 in x 30 in

Stephenson valve gear.

The original members of this class, introduced in 1928 by Collett, were rebuilds of a much earlier design which first appeared in 1903. Ten of these engines were reconstructed in 1938/9, becoming the 8100 class, and had a higher boiler pressure and 5 ft 6 in driving wheels. In 1929 new construction of the 5100 class began. These were sometimes referred to as the 5101 class, being of modified design. These versatile locomotives were to be found in many parts of the Western Region working on passenger and goods duties. Ten have survived.

5100 class no. 4112, photographed while lying at the back of Banbury shed, was at this time in a very unkempt condition. The letter D in a circle above the numberplate is the power class.

9.63

The 5100 class 2–6–2Ts were ideally suited to local passenger workings. No. 4159 is seen here arriving at Exeter St Thomas station.

4.9.56

Dumped at the back of Banbury repair shop, no. 5170 awaits the return of its trailing wheel set which had been removed for attention. Three of the 5100 class were normally allocated to this depot.

24.11.54

6100 class 2–6–2T 4MT

Designer: C.B. Collett.
Total built: 70.

Principal dimensions

Weight:	78 tons 9 cwt
Boiler Pressure:	225 lb/sq in (superheated)
Driving Wheels:	5 ft 8 in
Tractive Effort:	27,340 lb
Cylinders:	(0) 18 in x 30 in

Stephenson valve gear.

During the fifties there was a constant flow of these engines into and out of Paddington, working suburban services. Others could be seen employed as station pilots. The 6100 class was introduced in 1931 for this work. Seventy engines numbered 6100–69 were built between 1931 and 1935 and were a development by Collett of the earlier 5100 class. The 6100s had higher boiler pressure and tractive effort. No. 6106 is the only survivor and can be found at Didcot Railway Centre.

No. 6128 arrives at Paddington with a suburban service. During the fifties most of these engines were allocated to Old Oak Common, Slough, Southall, Reading and Oxford depots.

7.5.55

Six members of the 6100 class were allocated to Oxford. No. 6111 is pictured here at its home depot. The first locomotive of the class, no. 6100, was withdrawn in 1958.

31.10.54

Most of the 6100 class 2–6–2Ts spent their working days on London suburban work. When they were replaced by diesels they were to be found at many depots. No. 6113, formerly an Oxford engine, is seen here at Gloucester shed.

27.10.65

5600 class 0–6–2T 5MT

Designer: C.B. Collett.
Total built: 200.

Principal dimensions

Weight:	68 tons 12 cwt
Boiler Pressure:	200 lb/sq in (superheated)
Driving Wheels:	4 ft 7½ in
Tractive Effort:	25,800 lb
Cylinders:	18 in x 26 in

Stephenson valve gear.

The 5600 class was designed principally for use on the Welsh Valley lines where they handled both passenger and goods services. Introduced in 1924 to a Collett design, there were eventually two hundred locomotives built, with some detail alterations on the 1927 batch. Construction of the entire class took place over a four year period. The 5600s are well represented in preservation with nine examples at various railway centres.

5600 class no. 5655, seen here at Cardiff East Dock, was undergoing repairs to the middle set of driving wheels. The engine had been moved out into the shed yard and was also without a front numberplate.

30.8.55

Another 5600 class under repair is no. 5646 at Danygraig. Doubtless the fitter at the front of the engine would not mind working outside in the summer but it was a very different story in wintertime.

30.8.55

5600 class no. 6656 is pictured at Cohens Scrapyard, Kettering. This engine was an example of the second batch, nos. 6600–99, differing slightly from those in the 5600 series. In their final days many engines ran without numberplates. These were often replaced by hand painted numbers.

6.3.66

Rhymney Railway 0–6–2T 4F

Designer: H. Riches.

Principal dimensions

Weight:	66 tons
Boiler Pressure:	175 lb/sq in
Driving Wheels:	4 ft 6 in
Tractive Effort:	24,520 lb
Cylinders:	18½ in x 26 in

The locomotives originating from the smaller Welsh railway companies were rapidly being withdrawn in the early fifties. By 1955 only eight of the Rhymney Railway 0–6–2Ts were still in service, their numbers being halved the following year, finally becoming extinct in 1957. The remaining engines in 1955 were to be found at Cardiff East Dock shed. These locomotives were introduced in 1927 to a design by Harry Riches and known as the R1 class. They were a development of the much earlier R class introduced in 1907.

63

Cardiff East Dock shed with ex-Rhymney railway no. 36 ready to leave on duty 7, shunting in the dock area. In the background is one of the remaining Taff Vale Railway 0–6–2Ts. No. 36 was withdrawn from service in 1957.

30.8.55

In steam at the back of Cardiff East Docks shed is ex-Rhymney Railway no. 42. It is booked on duty 9 in the docks. No. 42 also was withdrawn in 1957.

30.8.55

Taff Vale 0–6–2T 4P

Designer: Great Western rebuilds of Cameron Taff Vale locomotives.

Principal dimensions

Weight:	65 tons 14 cwt
Boiler Pressure:	175 lb and 200 lb/sq in (superheated)
Driving Wheels:	5 ft 3 in
Tractive Effort:	21,000 lb
Cylinders:	$18\frac{1}{2}$ in x 26 in and $17\frac{1}{2}$ in x 26 in

The ex-Taff Vale Railway A class 0–6–2Ts had been steadily withdrawn from service during the early part of the fifties, and 1955 was the beginning of the end with forty making their final journey; the remaining fifteen followed in 1956, rendering the class extinct.

These engines were Great Western rebuilds of the Taff Vale engines introduced in 1924. During the rebuild they acquired superheated taper boilers and were fitted with vacuum brakes for passenger workings.

This picture of ex-Taff Vale no. 374 was taken at Cardiff East Dock just before it was withdrawn from service. Unfortunately, none of these engines has survived into preservation.

30.8.55

Another shot of no. 374 as it leaves Cardiff East Dock on one of its last duties. These engines were rebuilds of the Taff Vale A class with superheated taper Great Western type boilers.

30.8.55

Visitors to Swindon Works would almost certainly find several of the ex-Welsh railway engines present. Some of these were for overhaul, others were for scrap, a few of them spending a short time on works duties before being cut up. No. 344 is standing in the Works yard.

4.2.53

1361 class 0–6–0ST 0F

Designer: G.J. Churchward.
Total built: 5.

Principal dimensions

Weight:	35 tons 4 cwt
Boiler Pressure:	150 lb/sq in
Driving Wheels:	3 ft 8 in
Tractive Effort:	14,835 lb
Cylinders:	(0) 16 in x 20 in

Allan valve gear.

These sturdy 0–6–0STs were introduced by the Great Western Railway for dock shunting work in 1910 to a Churchward design. Four of the class were allocated to Plymouth Laira depot, with the fifth member at Taunton during the mid-fifties. Only one has survived, no. 1363, for many years one of the Plymouth engines.

Having replenished its coal and water supply, no. 1361 is ready to move off Plymouth Laira depot to resume shunting duties on the docks. This class was one of the few saddle tanks on the Western Region at this time as the vast majority of tanks were panniers.

4.9.56

1366 class 0–6–0PT 1F

Designer: C.B. Collett.
Total built: 6.

Principal dimensions

Weight:	35 tons 15 cwt
Boiler Pressure:	165 lb/sq in
Driving Wheels:	3 ft 8 in
Tractive Effort:	16,320 lb
Cylinders:	(0) 16 in x 20 in

Stephenson valve gear.

These six locomotives, a development of the 1361 class, were introduced by Collett in 1934. They also were built for dock shunting work and were fitted with pannier tanks. Several worked at Weymouth Quay. One, no. 1369, still survives.

Only one member of the 1366 class pannier tanks survived into preservation. No. 1369 is seen here in preservation days on the Dart Valley Railway. These engines were a development of the much earlier Churchward 1361 class and both types were designed for dock shunting work.

20.9.68

1500 class 0–6–0PT 4F

Designer: F.W. Hawksworth.
Total built: 10.

Principal dimensions

Weight:	58 tons 4 cwt
Boiler Pressure:	200 lb/sq in
Driving Wheels:	4 ft 7½ in
Tractive Effort:	22,515 lb
Cylinders:	(0) 17½ in x 24 in

Walschaerts valve gear – piston valves.

These powerful locomotives were built to a design by Hawksworth for heavy shunting duties. They first made their appearance in 1949 and ten were constructed, numbered 1500–09. During the fifties locomotives of this class could often be seen engaged in carriage pilot duties at Paddington, with half of the class being allocated to Old Oak Common depot. After withdrawal three were sold to the National Coal Board and used in the Coventry area. One of these, no. 1501, has survived into preservation and is currently undergoing restoration.

No. 1505 was photographed at Old Oak Common depot awaiting its next carriage pilot duty at Paddington. These locomotives were a familiar sight on these duties together with the 6100 class 2–6–2Ts.

7.8.55

1600 class 0–6–0PT 2F

Designer: F.W. Hawksworth.
Total built: 70.

Principal dimensions

Weight:	41 tons 12 cwt
Boiler Pressure:	165 lb/sq in
Driving Wheels:	4 ft 1½ in
Tractive Effort:	18,515 lb
Cylinders:	16½ in x 24 in

Stephenson valve gear.

   Seventy members of this class were built between 1949 and 1955 to a design by Hawksworth for light branch line and shunting duties. One has survived, no. 1638, built in 1951. During the mid-fifties a considerable number of these locomotives were to be found at depots in Wales.

No. 1634 was one of the two members of the 1600 class allocated to Danygraig depot during the mid-fifties. The engine was engaged on shunting work at Swansea docks when this picture was taken. Note the duty number 4 on the locomotive's buffer beam.

30.8.55

5400 class 0–6–0PT 1P

Designer: C.B. Collett.
Total built: 25.

Principal dimensions

Weight:	46 tons 12 cwt
Boiler Pressure:	165 lb/sq in
Driving Wheels:	5 ft 2 in
Tractive Effort:	14,780 lb
Cylinders:	$16\frac{1}{2}$ in x 24 in

This twenty-five-strong class, numbered 5400–24, was designed by Collett and introduced in 1931 for passenger work. They were push-pull fitted and were to be found at several Western Region depots. Rather surprisingly none has survived.

No. 5404 was one of three members of the class allocated to Banbury depot. This class was designed for light passenger duties and all were push-pull fitted.

27.3.55

Another of the Banbury 5400 class, no. 5407 is seen in steam outside the shed. The locomotive had just been coaled judging by the amount of coal lying on the cab roof.

27.3.55

5700 class 0–6–0PT 4F

Designer: C.B. Collett.
Total built: 863.

Principal dimensions

Weight:	47–50 tons
Boiler Pressure:	200 lb/sq in
Driving Wheels:	4 ft 7½ in
Tractive Effort:	22,515 lb
Cylinders:	17½ in x 24 in

Stephenson valve gear.

Over a twenty year period 863 examples of the standard pannier tank design were constructed. The first locomotive appeared in 1929 to a design by Collett. Although principally for light goods and shunting work these engines were often to be seen on passenger services and in use as carriage pilots. Some members of the class were fitted with steam brakes only. Eleven had condensing gear for working through the Metropolitan tunnels, otherwise (apart from cab variations) they were a very uniform class. When released from their usual duties by more modern motive power the panniers were to be seen in unfamiliar territory. The Folkestone branch and carriage duties at Clapham Junction were just two examples.

On withdrawal some of these locomotives were purchased by London Transport and the National Coal Board who used them at South Wales collieries.

The well known panniers are well represented in preservation with no less than sixteen examples, six of which were engines sold to London Transport.

72

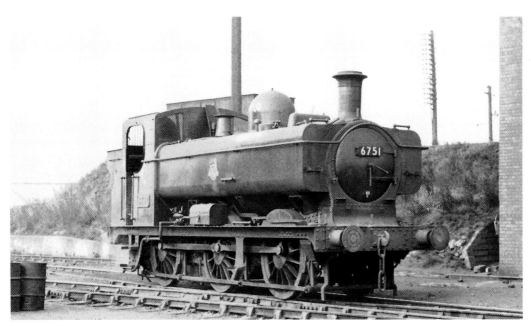

No. 6751 was photographed at Cardiff East Dock depot. This was one of the locomotives fitted with steam brakes only.

30.8.55

The 'Not to be Moved' signs were seen in use at many locomotive depots during the fifties. One of these has been placed on the buffer beam of no. 8720 as it stood outside Danygraig depot.

30.8.55

There was very little variation among the 863 examples of the 5700 class which was the Great Western, later Western Region, standard shunter. No. 3730 was one of the panniers allocated to Cardiff East Dock shed.

30.8.55

Pannier tanks of the 5700 class were often seen on branch passenger duties. No. 9669 of Brecon depot was on passenger work when this picture was taken at Bala.

27.6.62

The 5700 pannier tanks were built by a number of locomotive builders. No. 7751 was constructed by the North British Locomotive Company in 1930. The engine is seen here at Cardiff East Dock. Note the once familiar water crane and attendant solid fuel heating stove.

30.8.55

Eleven panniers were fitted with condensing gear for working through the tunnels of the Metropolitan line. No. 9704 was at Old Oak Common depot.

9.9.51

6400 class 0–6–0PT 2P/7400 class 0–6–0PT 2F

Designer: C.B. Collett.
Total built: 6400s – 40, 7400s – 50.

Principal dimensions

Weight:	45 tons
Boiler Pressure:	180 lb/sq in
Driving Wheels:	4 ft 7½ in
Tractive Effort:	18,010 lb
Cylinders:	16½ in x 24 in

Stephenson valve gear.

The 6400 was the first of these two classes to be introduced, the design being very similar to the 5400 class but with smaller wheels. They were push-pull fitted. The class was designed by Collett and introduced in 1932 with construction lasting for five years, during which time forty were built.

The 7400 class differed only in that they were not fitted for push-pull working. The first locomotive was constructed in 1936 and the last in 1950, with fifty locomotives comprising the class. Three of the 5400 class are in preservation but none of the 7400 class has survived.

No. 7411 stands at Oxford shed next to part of the depot's breakdown train. The fifty examples of the 7400 class were not fitted for push-pull working.

31.10.54

Despite this photograph being taken at Aberystwyth in 1961 the letters G W R can be clearly seen on the tank side of no. 7428. There is no visible trace of either British Railways lettering or the BR emblem.

7.61

Three 6400 class 0–6–0PTs have been preserved. No. 6412 is seen here at Buckfastleigh on the Dart Valley Railway. The class was introduced in 1932 to a Collett design for branch line work and all were push-pull fitted.

20.9.68

9400 class 0–6–0PT 4F

Designer: F.W. Hawksworth.
Total built: 210.

Principal dimensions

Weight:	55 tons 7 cwt
Boiler Pressure:	200 lb/sq in
Driving Wheels:	4 ft 7½ in
Tractive Effort:	22,515 lb
Cylinders:	17½ in x 24 in

Stephenson valve gear.

These heavy shunting locomotives were introduced in 1947, the year before railway nationalization. They were designed by Hawksworth, with the first ten being superheated. A further two hundred were built by private companies but these were not fitted with superheated boilers. All were delivered in BR days with the last batch of ten in 1956, making them the last Great Western design to be constructed. The class was numbered 9400–99, 8400–99 and 3400–09, and both of the surviving engines are from the first numbered series.

It was a busy time over the ash pits at Oxford depot as several tank locomotives arrived at the end of their working day. No. 8432 was one of the two members of the class allocated to the shed at this time.

29.4.56

No. 8431 is ready for its next duty at Cardiff East Dock shed. This engine was one of the batch built by outside contractors. Only the first ten members of the class were built at Swindon.

30.8.55

1400 class 0–4–2T 1P

Designer: C.B. Collett.
Total built: 75.

Principal dimensions

Weight:	41 tons 6 cwt
Boiler Pressure:	165 lb/sq in
Driving Wheels:	5 ft 2 in
Tractive Effort:	13,900 lb
Cylinders:	16 in x 24 in

Stephenson valve gear.

The Great Western Railway operated many branch lines and in 1932 Collett introduced the neat 1400 class 0–4–2Ts for this work. Seventy-five were constructed between 1932 and 1936 and all were push-pull fitted. The GWR AutoTrain with a 1400 class in charge soon became a familiar sight. In the fifties withdrawals commenced, line closures and diesel units quickly taking their toll. When this class was introduced it was known as the 4800 class but in 1946 they were renumbered to 1400–74. Four have survived into preservation.

Three of the 1400 class 0–4–2Ts were allocated to Oxford in the mid-fifties. Whenever one visited the depot at this time at least one would almost certainly be present. No. 1420 is one of the four lucky survivors.

29.4.56

Another of the trio of 1400s at Oxford was no. 1425. This engine was not as lucky as its shedmate. This class and the very similar 5800 class were the only 0–4–2T designs on the Western Region at this time.

27.2.55

5800 class 0–4–2T 1P

Designer: C.B. Collett.
Total built: 20.

Principal dimensions

Weight:	41 tons 6 cwt
Boiler Pressure:	165 lb/sq in
Driving Wheels:	5 ft 2 in
Tractive Effort:	13,900 lb
Cylinders:	16 in x 24 in

    These were identical locomotives to the well known 1400 class and were introduced in 1933. They were not push-pull fitted although built and used on branch line services. Withdrawals commenced in 1957 when their numbers were halved and only one lasted into the sixties. None has survived.

The 5800 class locomotives were identical to the more numerous 1400s, the only difference being that the twenty 5800s were not push-pull fitted although they were used on branch line duties. No. 5808 is seen here at Oxford.

29.4.56

1101 class 0–4–0T 3F

Designer: Avonside Engine Co.
Total built: 6.

Principal dimensions

Weight:	38 tons 4 cwt
Boiler Pressure:	170 lb/sq in
Driving Wheels:	3 ft 9½ in
Tractive Effort:	19,510 lb
Cylinders:	(0) 16 in x 24 in

Walschaerts valve gear.

The six engines of this class were built by the Avonside Engine Company of Bristol and were a short wheelbase design for dock shunting work. During the mid-fifties they were all allocated to Danygraig depot, a small shed with a total allocation of twenty-eight engines, all of which were tank designs. The class became extinct in 1960.

No. 1105 is seen busily shunting at Swansea Docks on duty no. 1. Note the warning bell fitted immediately in front of the cab. All six examples of this class were to be found at Danygraig shed.
30.8.55

Powlesland & Mason 0–4–0ST 0F

Designer: Pecketts, Bristol.

Principal dimensions

Weight:	33 tons 10 cwt
Boiler Pressure:	150 lb/sq in
Driving Wheels:	3 ft 7 in
Tractive Effort:	14,010 lb
Cylinders:	(0) 15 in x 21 in

Three locomotives built by Pecketts of Bristol for Powlesland & Mason Contractors were taken into Great Western stock, becoming nos. 1150–2. The first was withdrawn in 1952 but the others remained in service for several more years. They were of short wheelbase, typical Peckett design with added Great Western features and also fitted with a warning bell. One other ex-Powlesland & Mason 0–4–0ST, no. 1153 from Hawthorn Leslie, was withdrawn in 1955.

No. 1152 was built by Pecketts for Powlesland & Mason. It is seen here at Swansea East Dock shed. This depot had just thirty-five engines, all of tank designs, with many pannier tanks of 5700 and 9400 classes.

30.8.55

Vale of Rheidol Railway 2–6–2T Narrow Gauge

Total built: 3, all named.

Principal dimensions

Weight:	25 tons
Boiler Pressure:	165 lb/sq in
Driving Wheels:	2 ft 6 in
Tractive Effort:	9,615 lb and 10,150 lb
Cylinders:	11 in x 17 in and (0) 11½ in x 17 in (later engines)

Walschaerts valve gear.

7   *Owain Glyndwr*   8   *Llywelyn*   9   *Prince of Wales*

The three locomotives of this 1 ft 11½ in gauge line were destined to become the last to be operated by British Railways. Numbered 7, 8 and 9, they were responsible for services on the branch to Devil's Bridge for many years. No. 9 was built by Davies & Metcalfe for the Vale of Rheidol and completed in February 1902 while nos. 7 and 8 were built at Swindon Works in 1923 and were a development of the earlier design.

During the fifties all three engines were in standard green livery, fully lined out with lion and wheel crest on the tank side and brass cabside number and name plates. In addition they were fitted with a smokebox numberplate. In due course they received the unlined blue livery and carried the large BR logo on the tank side. All three engines survive in private ownership.

A well-loaded Aberystwyth to Devil's Bridge train is taking water en route. Locomotive no. 7 *Owain Glyndwr* was built at Swindon in 1923. Note the bucket which always seemed to be present on the locomotives' buffer beam.

9.9.65

This side view of Vale of Rheidol no. 8 *Llywelyn* was taken when the engines were still in BR green livery. Here the engine awaits departure time at Devil's Bridge. The Walschaerts valve gear fitted to these 2–6–2Ts can be clearly seen. No. 8 was built at Swindon in 1923.

15.7.59

The oldest of the three Vale of Rheidol 2–6–2Ts was no. 9, built by Davies & Metcalfe in 1902 and rebuilt at Swindon in 1923. No. 9 is seen here in unlined blue livery and with the BR logo in part of Aberystwyth station after modification for these particular trains.

15.6.68

Welshpool & Llanfair 0–6–0T

Designer: Beyer Peacock.
Total built: 2.

Principal dimensions

Weight:	19 tons 18 cwt
Boiler Pressure:	150 lb/sq in
Driving Wheels:	2 ft 9 in
Tractive Effort:	8,175 lb
Cylinders:	(0) 11½ in x 16 in

Walschaerts valve gear.

The two locomotives built for the 2 ft 6½ in gauge Welshpool and Llanfair section of the Cambrian Railways were taken into British Railways stock. Later they passed into private ownership and are still to be found at the railway.

Both engines were built in 1903 by Beyer Peacock, works nos. 3496–7. They carried Great Western, and later Western region, numbers 822–3. Both survive and are now numbered no. 1 *The Earl* and no. 2 *The Countess*.

The two 0–6–0Ts of the Welshpool & Llanfair Railway were built by Beyer Peacock in 1903. *The Earl* is seen here in unlined black livery in early preservation days; prior to this it was BR no. 822.

10.9.65

Resplendent in fully lined out livery *The Countess*, BR no. 823, is seen here as no. 2, its old Welshpool & Llanfair number, after restoration.

12.6.66

Additional Small Shunting Locomotives

Several other small 0–4–0ST tank locomotives were still in service during the mid-fifties (not illustrated). These were numbered and built as follows:

1140   Built in 1905 by Andrew Barclay
1142   Built in 1911 by Hudswell Clarke
1143   Built in 1908 by Peckett
1144   Built in 1909 by Hawthorn Leslie
1145   Built in 1918 by Peckett
1338   Built in 1898 by Kitson, rebuilt 1916

Nameplates

The Vale of Rheidol narrow gauge engines were repainted in BR blue during their final years before private purchase. No. 9 *Prince of Wales* is seen in this livery complete with the BR logo.

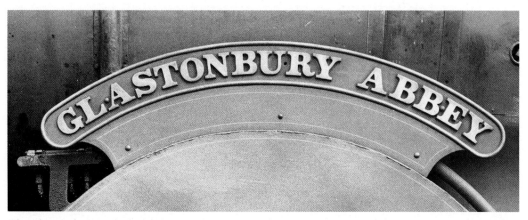

The 'Star' class included locomotives in several series, among them the 'Abbeys'. No. 4061 *Glastonbury Abbey* was one of the last engines of this class in service.

'Castle' class no. 7027 *Thornbury Castle* is one of the eight members of this class to survive. This picture of the nameplate was taken during the engine's final years in service.

'Castle' class no. 4037 *The South Wales Borderers* had a small badge below the nameplate which read *Egypt* with the letters *SWB* at the base.

One Great Western design that completely slipped through the preservation net was the eighty-strong 'Grange' class. These were very similar to the 'Halls' but with smaller driving wheels. This picture is of the nameplate of no. 6874 *Haughton Grange*.

SOUTHERN REGION

MN 'Merchant Navy' class 4–6–2 8P

Designer: O.V. Bulleid.
Total built: 30, all named.

Principal dimensions (rebuilt engines)

Weight:	Locomotive	97³/₄ tons
Boiler Pressure:		280 lb/sq in
Driving Wheels:		6 ft 2 in
Tractive Effort:		33,490 lb
Cylinders:		(3) 18 in x 24 in

Walschaerts valve gear.

35001	*Channel Packet*	35016	*Elders Fyffes*
35002	*Union Castle*	35017	*Belgian Marine*
35003	*Royal Mail*	35018	*British India Line*
35004	*Cunard White Star*	35019	*French Line CGT*
35005	*Canadian Pacific*	35020	*Bibby Line*
35006	*Peninsular & Oriental S.N.Co.*	35021	*New Zealand Line*
35007	*Aberdeen Commonwealth*	35022	*Holland–America Line*
35008	*Orient Line*	35023	*Holland–Afrika Line*
35009	*Shaw Savill*	35024	*East Asiatic Company*
35010	*Blue Star*	35025	*Brocklebank Line*
35011	*General Steam Navigation*	35026	*Lamport & Holt Line*
35012	*United States Line*	35027	*Port Line*
35013	*Blue Funnel*	35028	*Clan Line*
35014	*Nederland Line*	35029	*Ellerman Lines*
35015	*Rotterdam Lloyd*	35030	*Elder Dempster Lines*

The Merchant Navy class locomotives, with their air-smoothed casing, were introduced in 1941 to the design of O.V. Bulleid, Chief Mechanical Engineer of the Southern Railway, and, after a few initial problems, they revolutionized the express passenger locomotive classes of the Southern Railway. They included features new to British practice such as welded steel fireboxes, 280 lb/sq in pressure, power-operated firedoors and box section wheels. In all thirty members of the class were constructed at Eastleigh Works, the last being completed in April 1949. Rebuilding commenced in late 1955 with the first rebuild appearing early in the following year and all were completed by 1959. The final form greatly improved their performance, economy and servicing. Several of the Merchant Navy class were to remain active until steam operation ceased in the region. One example, no. 35028 *Clan Line*, was to be purchased on withdrawal. The first to be condemned were no. 35002 *Union Castle* and no. 35015 *Rotterdam Lloyd* in February 1964, sold to scrap dealers at Rotherham and cut up. Others were to follow to several other companies. In all eleven locomotives of the class have survived, several of which are fully restored.

'Merchant Navy' no. 35004 *Cunard White Star* photographed at its home shed, Exmouth Junction (72A). This engine was rebuilt in July 1958 and withdrawn in October 1965, ending its days under the cutting torch at Eastleigh shed early the following year.

4.9.56

'Merchant Navy' no. 35020 *Bibby Line*, rebuilt a few months prior to this photograph being taken, at Waterloo heading 'The Atlantic Coast Express'. This engine was withdrawn in February 1965 and broken up by the Southern Region.

3.9.56

'Merchant Navy' no. 35024 *East Asiatic Company* photographed at Nine Elms prior to working back to its home shed, Exmouth Junction. This engine was rebuilt in April 1959 and withdrawn from service in January 1965. It ended its days at a Newport scrapyard.

12.7.54

'Merchant Navy' no. 35026 *Lamport & Holt Line* turns at Folkestone shed after working a boat train. Rebuilding of this locomotive was completed in February 1957 and on withdrawal in April 1967 it was sent to Cashmores of Newport and cut up.

3.7.53

'West Country' & 'Battle of Britain' classes 4–6–2 6MT

Designer: O.V. Bulleid.
Total built: 110.

Principal dimensions (Rebuilt locomotives)

Weight:	Locomotive	86 tons
Boiler Pressure:		250 lb/sq in
Driving Wheels:		6 ft 2 in
Tractive Effort:		27,720 lb
Cylinders:		(3) $16^{3}/_{8}$ in x 24 in

Bulleid valve gear (rebuilds Walschaerts).

34001	*Exeter*	34035	*Shaftesbury*
34002	*Salisbury*	34036	*Westward Ho*
34003	*Plymouth*	34037	*Clovelly*
34004	*Yeovil*	34038	*Lynton*
34005	*Barnstaple*	34039	*Boscastle*
34006	*Bude*	34040	*Crewkerne*
34007	*Wadebridge*	34041	*Wilton*
34008	*Padstow*	34042	*Dorchester*
34009	*Lyme Regis*	34043	*Combe Martin*
34010	*Sidmouth*	34044	*Woolacombe*
34011	*Tavistock*	34045	*Ottery St Mary*
34012	*Launceston*	34046	*Braunton*
34013	*Okehampton*	34047	*Callington*
34014	*Budleigh Salterton*	34048	*Crediton*
34015	*Exmouth*	34049	*Anti-Aircraft Command*
34016	*Bodmin*	34050	*Royal Observer Corps*
34017	*Ilfracombe*	34051	*Winston Churchill*
34018	*Axminster*	34052	*Lord Dowding*
34019	*Bideford*	34053	*Sir Keith Park*
34020	*Seaton*	34054	*Lord Beaverbrook*
34021	*Dartmoor*	34055	*Fighter Pilot*
34022	*Exmoor*	34056	*Croydon*
34023	*Blackmore Vale*	35057	*Biggin Hill*
34024	*Tamar Valley*	35058	*Sir Frederick Pile*
34025	*Whimple*	35059	*Sir Archibald Sinclair*
34026	*Yes Tor*	35060	*25 Squadron*
34027	*Taw Valley*	34061	*73 Squadron*
34028	*Eddystone*	34062	*17 Squadron*
34029	*Lundy*	34063	*229 Squadron*
34030	*Watersmeet*	34064	*Fighter Command*
34031	*Torrington*	34065	*Hurricane*
34032	*Camelford*	34066	*Spitfire*
34033	*Chard*	34067	*Tangmere*
34034	*Honiton*	34068	*Kenley*

34069	*Hawkinge*	34090	*Sir Eustace Missenden, Southern Railway*
34070	*Manston*	34091	*Weymouth*
34071	*601 Squadron*	34092	*City of Wells*
34072	*257 Squadron*	34093	*Saunton*
34073	*249 Squadron*	34094	*Mortehoe*
34074	*46 Squadron*	34095	*Brentor*
34075	*264 Squadron*	34096	*Trevone*
34076	*41 Squadron*	34097	*Holsworthy*
34077	*603 Squadron*	34098	*Templecombe*
34078	*222 Squadron*	34099	*Lynmouth*
34079	*141 Squadron*	34100	*Appledore*
34080	*74 Squadron*	34101	*Hartland*
34081	*92 Squadron*	34102	*Lapford*
34082	*615 Squadron*	34103	*Calstock*
34083	*605 Squadron*	34104	*Bere Alston*
34084	*253 Squadron*	34105	*Swanage*
34085	*501 Squadron*	34106	*Lydford*
34086	*219 Squadron*	34107	*Blandford Forum*
34087	*145 Squadron*	34108	*Wincanton*
34088	*213 Squadron*	34109	*Sir Trafford Leigh-Mallory*
34089	*602 Squadron*	34110	*66 Squadron*

The first of the 'West Country' light Pacifics was completed at Brighton Works in May 1945. These and the 'Battle of Britain' class were eventually to total 110 locomotives and both classes were identical except for their names. The last engine was completed in January 1951. All were built at Brighton except six which were constructed at Eastleigh Works.

Designed by Bulleid for the Southern Railway, they were originally streamlined and incorporated many of the features of the 'Merchant Navy' class locomotives. They were designed to replace elderly locomotives on West Country routes and to provide more powerful locomotives on the Eastern section. Eventually they were to become familiar on many Southern Region routes.

Rebuilding of the class commenced in 1957 with no. 34005 *Barnstaple* being the first to receive attention. In all sixty were rebuilt. Withdrawals commenced in 1963 with the non-rebuilds and the first of the rebuilds was withdrawn in the following year. Some of the early withdrawals were cut up by Eastleigh Works but the vast majority went to privately owned scrap yards. Fortunately, a number were to end up at Barry and in all twenty have survived. No. 34051 *Winston Churchill* is part of the National Collection, several others have been restored to working order and more are in the process of restoration or awaiting attention.

No. 34048 *Crediton* of Brighton shed stands ready for its next duty at Salisbury. This locomotive was rebuilt in March 1959, remaining in service until March 1966 when it was sent to Cashmores of Newport and cut up.

3.9.56

Another member of the 'West Country' class, no. 34045 *Ottery St Mary*, is seen at Eastleigh shed. This locomotive was rebuilt in October 1958 and withdrawn from service in June 1964.

8.11.55

'Battle of Britain' class no. 34062 *17 Squadron* standing outside its home shed, Exmouth Junction. This engine was rebuilt in April 1959 and remained in service until June 1964. Note the squadron crest below the nameplate.

4.9.55

The light Bulleid Pacifics were a familiar sight at Salisbury. No. 34049 *Anti-Aircraft Command* was completed at Eastleigh in December 1946 and rebuilt in March 1959, after which it remained in service until December 1963 and was cut up at its birthplace in June 1964.

3.9.56

'West Country' class no. 34093 *Saunton* was rebuilt in May 1960. When this picture was taken at Weymouth the locomotive had lost its nameplates. Several of the Bulleid Pacifics ran without these in the final months of service. No. 34093 was withdrawn in July 1967 and was to spend several months stored at Weymouth before ending its days at Cashmores in Newport.

14.9.66

'West Country' no. 34023 *Blackmore Vale* is one of the lucky survivors. This picture of the locomotive was taken at Weymouth motive power depot. *Blackmore Vale* was not rebuilt and following withdrawal from service in July 1967 it spent a short period in store. It is now to be found at the Bluebell Railway.

14.9.66

By 1967 many of the Bulleid Pacifics remaining in service were running without name and front numberplates. No. 34060 *25 Squadron* pictured at Bournemouth depot has its front number painted on. Despite this these engines were still in regular use on express trains. No. 34060 was withdrawn in July 1967 and cut up at Cashmores in Newport the following year.

12.3.67

H15 class 4–6–0 4MT

Designer: R.W. Urie/R.E.L. Maunsell.

Principal dimensions

Weight:	Locomotive	79–82 tons (depending on type)
Boiler Pressure:		175 or 180 lb/sq in (depending on type)
Driving Wheels:		6 ft
Tractive Effort:		26,240 lb (with variations)
Cylinders:		21 in x 28 in

Walschaerts valve gear – piston valves.

Under this classification were to be found a mixture of engines. The oldest examples were designed by Urie for the London & South Western Railway and introduced in 1914. In the following year the rebuilds of a 1907 Drummond 4–6–0 appeared. In 1924 Maunsell introduced the locomotives with the N15 type boiler and his rebuilds of earlier Drummond 4–6–0s. One of the type to appear in 1927 was a rebuild of a Urie loco with an N15 type boiler.

The H15s were mixed traffic engines and used on passenger, parcels and goods workings. The last members of the H15 class were withdrawn in December 1961 and none has been preserved.

Several H15 class locomotives were allocated to Nine Elms depot in the fifties and others were frequent visitors. No. 30477 was an Eastleigh engine, one of the Maunsell design introduced in 1924. This engine was withdrawn in 1959.

12.7.54

Another example of the Maunsell H15 locomotives, no. 30478 was also an Eastleigh engine, photographed here at its home depot. These locomotives were very similar to the 'King Arthur' class in appearance. No. 30478 lasted until 1959.

23.11.54

H15 class no. 30331 was one of the batch introduced in 1924. These were rebuilds by Maunsell of Drummond 4–6–0s. No. 30331 was a Salisbury engine. The majority of this type were withdrawn between 1956 and 1958 except no. 30331 which lasted until 1961. The locomotive is being made ready to leave Eastleigh shed.

8.11.55

'Lord Nelson' class 4–6–0 6P

Designer: R.E.L. Maunsell.
Total built: 16, all named.

Principal dimensions

Weight:	Locomotive	83 tons 10 cwt
Boiler Pressure:		220 lb/sq in
Driving Wheels:		6 ft 7 in (6 ft 3 in for no. 30859)
Tractive Effort:		33,510 lb (35,300 lb for no. 30859)
Cylinders:		(4) 16½ in x 26 in

Walschaerts valve gear – piston valves.
No. 30860 was fitted with longer boiler.

30850	*Lord Nelson*		30858	*Lord Duncan*
30851	*Sir Francis Drake*		30859	*Lord Hood*
30852	*Sir Walter Raleigh*		30860	*Lord Hawke*
30853	*Sir Richard Grenville*		30861	*Lord Anson*
30854	*Howard of Effingham*		30862	*Lord Collingwood*
30855	*Robert Blake*		30863	*Lord Rodney*
30856	*Lord St Vincent*		30864	*Sir Martin Frobisher*
30857	*Lord Howe*		30865	*Sir John Hawkins*

This class consisted of sixteen locomotives built to a design by Maunsell for the Southern Railway. The first example appeared in 1926 with the last member of the class being constructed in 1929. Several modifications, considerably altering their appearance, were made over the years, including smokebox deflectors, double blastpipes and wide chimneys.

These engines were principal express locomotives in their heyday. In later years they were often to be found heading semi-fast passenger trains. Fortunately no. 30850 *Lord Nelson* has survived into preservation.

'Lord Nelson' no. 30851 *Sir Francis Drake* was photographed at Eastleigh depot, its home shed. Many of the class finished their days allocated to this depot.

8.11.55

The distinctive large chimney and smoke deflectors fitted to the 'Lord Nelson' class locomotives can be clearly seen in this picture of no. 30861 *Lord Anson*, a Bournemouth depot engine receiving attention over Nine Elms ashpits.

24.5.56

'Lord Nelson' no. 30852 *Sir Walter Raleigh* is seen at the head of a fast passenger train awaiting departure time at Eastleigh. In their later years they were relegated to this work although they were occasionally still to be seen heading expresses.

9.11.55

N15 'King Arthur' class 4–6–0 5P

These engines and the 'Lord Nelson' class were the principal Southern Railway express passenger locomotives in the pre-war period, many of their duties being later taken over by Bulleid Pacifics.
Designer: R.W. Urie/R.E.L. Maunsell.
Total built: 74, all named.

Principal dimensions (original batch)

Weight:	Locomotive	80 tons 7 cwt
Boiler Pressure:		180 lb/sq in (superheated)
Driving Wheels:		6 ft 7 in
Tractive Effort:		26,245 lb
Cylinders:		(0) 22 in x 28 in

Walschaerts valve gear – piston valves.
Other batches had boiler pressure of 200 lb/sq in, different cylinder sizes and different tractive effort.

30448	*Sir Tristram*		30452	*Sir Meliagrance*
30449	*Sir Torre*		30453	*King Arthur*
34050	*Sir Kay*		30454	*Queen Guinevere*
30451	*Sir Lamorak*		30455	*Sir Launcelot*

102

30456	Sir Galahad	30774	Sir Gaheris
30457	Sir Bedivere	30775	Sir Agravaine
30736	Excalibur	30776	Sir Galagars
30737	King Uther	30777	Sir Lamiel
0738	King Pellinore	30778	Sir Pelleas
30739	King Leodegrance	30779	Sir Colgrevance
30740	Merlin	30780	Sir Persant
30741	Joyous Gard	30781	Sir Aglovale
30742	Camelot	30782	Sir Brian
30743	Lyonnesse	30783	Sir Gillemere
30744	Maid of Astolat	30784	Sir Nerovens
30745	Tintagel	30785	Sir Mador de la Porte
30746	Pendragon	30786	Sir Lionel
30747	Elaine	30787	Sir Menadeuke
30748	Vivien	30788	Sir Urre of the Mount
30749	Iseult	30789	Sir Guy
30750	Morgan le Fay	30790	Sir Villiars
30751	Etarre	30791	Sir Uwaine
30752	Linette	30792	Sir Hervis de Reve
30753	Melisande	30793	Sir Ontzlake
30754	The Green Knight	30794	Sir Ector de Maris
30755	The Red Knight	30795	Sir Dinadan
30763	Sir Bors de Ganis	30796	Sir Dodinas le Savage
30764	Sir Gawin	30797	Sir Blamor de Ganis
30765	Sir Gareth	30798	Sir Hectimere
30766	Sir Geraint	30799	Sir Ironside
30767	Sir Valence	30800	Sir Meleaus de Lile
30768	Sir Balin	30801	Sir Meliot de Logres
30769	Sir Balan	30802	Sir Durnore
30770	Sir Prianius	30803	Sir Harry le Fise Lake
30771	Sir Sagramore	30804	Sir Cador of Cornwall
30772	Sir Percivale	30805	Sir Constantine
30773	Sir Lavaine	30806	Sir Galleron

The first of the 'King Arthur' class emerged from Eastleigh Works in August 1918 to the design of Urie for the London & South Western Railway. This was the first of several batches of these locomotives to be constructed. In 1925 the Maunsell engines with long travel valves, increased boiler pressure and smaller fireboxes appeared, others being introduced at this time with cabs modified for the Eastern section. The following year more were built for the Central section fitted with six-wheeled tenders.

Five locomotives of the original batch were fitted in the early forties with multiple jet blastpipes and large diameter chimneys, considerably altering their appearance. The first of the original locomotives was condemned in 1953 with the last of these twenty locomotives being withdrawn in March 1958. Withdrawals of the class increased from this time and the last remaining examples were condemned in 1962.

Only one 'King Arthur' has survived into preservation. This is no. 30777 Sir Lamiel which has become very well known, having been seen in action in many parts of the country.

'King Arthur' class no. 30747 *Elaine* is seen shunting at Eastleigh. Built in 1922, this was one of the original batch and remained in service until October 1956.

9.11.55

Several 'King Arthurs' were allocated to Eastleigh in the early fifties and others were frequent visitors. No. 30764 *Sir Gawin* was one of the 1925 introduction for the Eastern section with modified cab and eight-wheeled tender. This engine was withdrawn in July 1961.

8.11.55

'King Arthur' no. 30800 *Sir Meleaus de Lile* was one of the batch built for the Central section and transferred elsewhere on electrification. The engine, which was a Bricklayers Arms locomotive at this time, is seen here at Ashford. Note the straight sided tender.

14.5.55

No. 30776 *Sir Galagars* is seen at Dover shed ready to work an express. Six locomotives of the class were allocated to the depot at this time including the sole survivor no. 30777 *Sir Lamiel*.

3.7.53

The fitting of multiple jet blastpipes and large diameter chimney to no. 30755 *The Red Knight* and four others in 1940 considerably altered their appearance. No. 30755 was awaiting attention at Eastleigh Works when this picture was taken. *The Red Knight* was withdrawn in May 1957 and cut up at Eastleigh in the same month.

8.11.55

N15X 'Remembrance' class 4–6–0 4P

Introduced in 1934 by Maunsell for the Southern Railway, these locomotives were rebuilds of the class 4–6–4T of the London Brighton & South Coast Railway introduced in 1914.
Designer: R.E.L. Maunsell (rebuilds of LBSCR 4–6–4Ts).
Total built: 7, all named.

Principal dimensions

Weight:	Locomotive	73 tons 2 cwt
Boiler Pressure:		180 lb/sq in
Driving Wheels:		6 ft 9 in
Tractive Effort:		23,325 lb
Cylinders:		(0) 21 in x 28 in

Walschaerts valve gear – piston valves.

32327	*Trevithick*		32331	*Beattie*
32328	*Hackworth*		32332	*Stroudley*
32329	*Stephenson*		32333	*Remembrance*
32330	*Cudworth*			

In their final years all seven were allocated to Basingstoke depot and were employed on semi-fast passenger services to London. As a result they were often to be seen at Waterloo or being serviced at Nine Elms depot. The entire class was scrapped between 1955 and 1957.

No. 32328 *Hackworth* is turned at Nine Elms depot ready to work back to its home shed, Basingstoke, with a semi-fast passenger train. All seven members of this class ended their days working from this depot on these duties.

12.7.54

S15 class 4–6–0 6P

Designer: R.W. Urie/R.E.L. Maunsell.
Total built: 45.

Principal dimensions

Weight:	Locomotive	79 tons 16 cwt (with variations on last two batches)
Boiler Pressure:		180 lb/sq in
		200 lb/sq in (Maunsell engines)
Driving Wheels:		5 ft 7 in
Tractive Effort:		28,200 lb
		29,855 lb (Maunsell engines)
Cylinders:		(0) 21 in x 28 in
		(0) 20½ in x 28 in (Maunsell engines)

Walschaerts valve gear – piston valves.
Number series 30496–515 and 30823–47.

The S15 class was a development of the N15 'King Arthur' class designed by Urie for mixed traffic work on the London & South Western Railway and introduced in 1920. The original twenty locomotives were built at Eastleigh during 1920 and 1921 and were followed by another fifteen constructed in 1927 and 1928, with a final batch of ten built in 1936. The last two batches were built to a modified design by Maunsell at Eastleigh. The later engines had a higher boiler pressure, modified footplating, different cylinder size and other detail differences.

107

S15 no. 30506 at Feltham depot. This shed had a considerable number of the class in its allocation. This engine is one of two examples of the original Urie design to survive into preservation. Note the eight-wheeled tender fitted.

12.7.54

S15 no. 30499 stands in company with another member of the class at Feltham shed. This is the other lucky survivor of the first batch of S15s. Both examples are in preservation on the Watercress Line.

12.7.54

S15 no. 30841 was one of the batch introduced by Maunsell in 1927 and was built at Eastleigh in 1936; it is seen here at the famous Barry scrapyard. It was to prove lucky for this engine as it was in due course rescued and is now to be found at the North Yorkshire Moors Railway.

25.10.65

H2 class 4–4–2 4P

The H2 class were built in 1911/2 to the design of Marsh for the London Brighton & South Coast Railway. They were a superheated development of the H1 class with larger cylinders. These engines were very similar in appearance to the famous 'Great Northern Atlantics'.
Designer: D.E. Marsh.
Total built: 6.

Principal dimensions

Weight:	Locomotive	68 tons 2 cwt
Boiler Pressure:		200 lb/sq in (superheated)
Driving Wheels:		6 ft 7½ in
Tractive Effort:		24,520 lb
Cylinders:		(0) 21 in x 26 in
Piston valves.		

32421	*South Foreland*	32425	*Trevose Head*
32422	*North Foreland*	32426	*St. Alban's Head*
32424	*Beachy Head*		

In 1955 five of the famous 'Brighton Atlantics' remained in service, all allocated to Brighton and Newhaven. Time was running out as four were withdrawn in 1956 leaving no. 32424 to soldier on until it too disappeared in 1958. At this time it was the last Atlantic to run in normal revenue service. It would have made a splendid subject for preservation but it was not so fortunate.

H2 class no. 32421 *South Foreland* was one of the famous 'Brighton Atlantics'. When this picture was taken it was at its home shed Brighton. No. 32421 was withdrawn with three others in 1956.

25.6.55

D class 4–4–0 1P

Designer: H.S. Wainwright.
Total built: 51.

Principal dimensions

Weight:	Locomotive	50 tons
Boiler Pressure:		175 lb/sq in
Driving Wheels:		6 ft 8 in
Tractive Effort:		17,450 lb
Cylinders:		19 in x 26 in

Stephenson valve gear.

H.S. Wainwright, Chief Mechanical Engineer of the South Eastern & Chatham Railway, introduced the first of the D class 4–4–0s in 1901, an elegant design with round topped boiler and curved splashers. In the years up to 1907 a total of fifty-one were built. From 1921 Maunsell rebuilt twenty-one to become D1 class, these having superheated Belpaire boilers and long travel piston valves. At nationalization twenty-nine of the unrebuilt engines came into BR stock.

Fortunately, one example, no. 31737, has been retained as part of the National Collection. This engine was built at Ashford works in 1901.

Resplendent in lined BR black livery D class no. 31574 stands in the yard of its home shed, Ashford. All but one of the unrebuilt engines were taken into British Railways stock.

14.5.55

Ashford shed had a vacuum-operated turntable. Here we see the other side of no. 31574 as it prepares to move off after turning. Note the coal stacked high on the tender.

14.5.55

This side view of D class no. 31574 shows clearly the graceful lines of this design. The Ds generally spent much of their final years on local passenger work, although one could often be seen engaged in shunting operations at Ashford.

14.5.55

D1 class 4–4–0 2P

Designer: R.E.L. Maunsell.
Total built: 21.

Principal dimensions

Weight:	Locomotive	52 tons 4 cwt
Boiler Pressure:		180 lb/sq in (superheated)
Driving Wheels:		6 ft 8 in
Tractive Effort:		17,950 lb
Cylinders:		19 in x 26 in

These locomotives were rebuilds of the Wainwright D class introduced in 1901, the first of them appearing in 1921. They had superheated Belpaire boilers and long travel piston valves. The class consisted of twenty-one locomotives, rebuilding taking place at Ashford Works or Beyer Peacock & Co., with the last completed in 1927. All but one were taken into British Railways stock. They were principally used on both Eastern and Central sections handling heavy semi-fast and on occasions express trains right up until electrification of the former section. None has survived.

Awaiting attention in the repair shop at Bricklayers Arms, D1 no. 31741 was one of the locomotives rebuilt at Ashford Works in 1927. This engine remained in service until September 1959.

1.11.51

Although several D1 class 4–4–0s had been withdrawn, some of the survivors were still receiving full general overhaul and repainting at Ashford Works. No. 31727 was among a line of engines just brought over from the works by R1 class 0–6–0T no. 31147. No. 31727 was rebuilt from a D class at Ashford Works in 1922.

14.5.55

D15 class 4–4–0 3P

Designer: D. Drummond.
Total built: 10.

Principal dimensions

Weight:	Locomotive	61 tons 11 cwt
Boiler Pressure:		180 lb/sq in
Driving Wheels:		6 ft 7 in
Tractive Effort:		20,140 lb
Cylinders:		20 in x 26 in

Walschaerts valve gear – piston valves.

February 1912 was to see the first Drummond D15 class locomotive completed at Eastleigh Works. The remaining nine members of the class followed at fairly regular intervals throughout the year, the last example being completed in December. The entire class was later superheated by Urie. Withdrawals commenced in 1951 with six members of the class. The last two survivors were based at Nine Elms, nos. 30465 and 30467 working on semi-fast passenger services and empty stock workings. These two engines were condemned in January 1956 and September 1955 respectively.

D15 class no. 30467, one of the two allocated to Nine Elms, stands in the shed yard. This engine was built at Eastleigh in July 1912 and withdrawn in September 1955 and cut up at Ashford Works.
12.7.54

This picture of D15 no. 30465 shows the rather open cab of this class. This engine was in fully lined black livery and is standing among the engines destined for Eastleigh Works.

5.11.55

Time was running out for D15 class no. 30465 when it was photographed at Eastleigh, as this engine was the sole survivor of the class at this time. It was withdrawn just two months later and cut up at Brighton Works.

5.11.55

E class 4–4–0 1P

Designer: H.S. Wainwright.
Total built: 26.

Principal dimensions

Weight:	Locomotive	52 tons 5 cwt
Boiler Pressure:		180 lb/sq in
Driving Wheels:		6 ft 6 in
Tractive Effort:		18,410 lb
Cylinders:		19 in x 26 in

The E class 4–4–0 designed by Wainwright for the South Eastern & Chatham Railway just made it into 1955. With the withdrawal of no. 31166 this class became extinct. Of the twenty-six locomotives built, eleven were rebuilt as E1 class which considerably altered their appearance. The first of the E class was completed in 1905 and the last in 1909.

The last survivor was allocated to Tonbridge depot.

The last survivor of the graceful E class, no. 31166 stands in the yard at Ashford Works awaiting its fate. Note that the tender was still lettered 'British Railways'.

14–5–55

E1 class 4–4–0 1P

Designer: R.E.L. Maunsell.
Total built: 11.

Principal dimensions

Weight:	Locomotive	53 tons 9 cwt
Boiler Pressure:		180 lb/sq in (superheated)
Driving Wheels:		6 ft 6 in
Tractive Effort:		18,410 lb
Cylinders:		19 in x 26 in

In 1919 Maunsell introduced the first of the rebuilds of the elegant E class. They had a larger superheated Belpaire boiler and long travel piston valves. In all eleven were rebuilt, all but one by Beyer Peacock & Co. in 1920/1. The odd one was rebuilt at Ashford Works in 1919. All were taken into BR stock with the first to go, no. 31162, in May 1949. By the mid-fifties seven remained in service. These engines were used on similar turns to the D1 rebuilds. Although three survived well into the sixties none is in preservation.

E1 class no. 31165 was in the process of receiving an intermediate overhaul at Ashford Works when this picture was taken. The seven E1 class 4–4–0s were rebuilds of the Wainwright E class. No. 31165 was rebuilt by Beyer Peacock & Co. in 1920 and withdrawn in May 1959.

14.5.55

117

In their heyday the E1 4–4–0s would have been seen on heavy express trains to the Kent Coast. By the fifties they were mostly on semi-fast and local services. No. 31067 was pictured at Bricklayers Arms. This engine was rebuilt from an E class in February 1920 by Beyer Peacock & Co.

25.11.54

L class 4–4–0 2P

Designer: H.S. Wainwright.
Total built: 22.

Principal dimensions

Weight:	Locomotive	57 tons 9 cwt
Boiler Pressure:		160 lb/sq in (superheated)
Driving Wheels:		6 ft 8 in
Tractive Effort:		18,575 lb
Cylinders:		$20\frac{1}{2}$ in x 26 in
Piston valves.		

This was the last 4–4–0 design by Wainwright for the South Eastern & Chatham Railway and was introduced in 1914. The class received various detail alterations in Southern Railway days. Twenty-two examples went into service, numbered 31760–81, with a considerable number allocated to Tonbridge and Ashford. None has survived into preservation.

One of Tonbridge shed's batch of L class 4–4–0s, no. 31760 received attention to its pistons outside the shed. Note the once familiar 'not to be moved' sign on the side of the smokebox. Small repairs such as this were often done outside owing to space problems.

1.7.53

L class no. 31773 had recently received Works attention and was running with a tender that was not carrying either the BR emblem or lettering. This engine was at its home shed, Tonbridge.

1.7.53

The graceful lines of L class no. 31772 are seen to advantage in this picture taken at Ashford. The L class was the last 4–4–0 design introduced by H.S. Wainwright for the SECR.

14.5.55

L1 class 4–4–0 2P

Designer: R.E.L. Maunsell.
Total built: 15.

Principal dimensions

Weight:	Locomotive	57 tons 16 cwt
Boiler Pressure:		180 lb/sq in (superheated)
Driving Wheels:		6 ft 8 in
Tractive Effort:		18,910 lb
Cylinders:		19½ in x 26 in

These post-grouping developments of the L class did not make their appearance until 1926. Among the modifications were long travel valves and side window cabs. Nearly half of this fifteen-strong class were to be found at Bricklayers Arms depot in the early fifties, their duties including semi-fasts and specials on the South Eastern section. Although most survived into the sixties none has been lucky enough to be preserved, as is unfortunately the case with many of the 4–4–0 designs of all regions.

Several of the L1 class 4–4–0s introduced by Maunsell in 1926 were allocated to Bricklayers Arms depot in London in the early fifties. One of these was no. 31785 seen here just leaving the depot. The first members of the fifteen-strong class were withdrawn in 1959.

25.11.54

T9 class 4–4–0 2P

Designer: D. Drummond.
Total built: 66.

Principal dimensions

Weight:	Locomotive	51 tons
Boiler Pressure:		175 lb/sq in (superheated)
Driving Wheels:		6 ft 7 in
Tractive Effort:		17,675 lb
Cylinders:		19 in x 26 in

Stephenson valve gear.

These very useful locomotives designed by Drummond for the LSWR were commonly known as 'Greyhounds' in their heyday and were used on principal expresses. It was in their later superheated form that these engines performed their finest work. In all sixty-six locomotives were built by Dubs & Co. and Nine Elms Works, the first appearing in 1899 and the last in October 1901. All survived to be taken into British Railways stock. Fifteen members of the class were converted to oil burning in 1947 but although successful this experiment was short-lived as within a year most were stored, never to work again and they were condemned in 1951. Withdrawals of the other class members commenced the following year. The final example in service was no. 30120 which had been restored to LSWR livery and carried the number 120. This engine is part of the National Collection and has been seen in action on BR and preserved railways over the years.

In their final years the T9s were often to be seen on cross country services and parcel trains with a number allocated in the West Country during the 1950s working to Padstow and on other lines. No. 30301 seen here at Salisbury was built at Nine Elms Works in 1900 and remained in service until withdrawn from this depot in August 1959. It ended its days at Ashford Works.

3.9.56

No. 30719 was a Nine Elms engine for a number of years before transfer in June 1959 to Exmouth Junction where it was to spend its final years. No. 30719 was built by Dubs & Co. in 1899. When this picture was taken it was receiving attention at Brighton Works and it was to remain in service until March 1961 before being cut up at Eastleigh the following month.

25.6.55

V 'Schools' class 4–4–0 5P

Designer: R.E.L. Maunsell.
Total built: 40, all named.

Principal dimensions

Weight:	Locomotive	67 tons 2 cwt
Boiler Pressure:		220 lb/sq in (superheated)
Driving Wheels:		6 ft 7 in
Tractive Effort:		25,135 lb
Cylinders:		(3) 16½ in x 26 in

Walschaerts valve gear – piston valves.

30900	*Eton*		30920	*Rugby*
30901	*Winchester*		30921	*Shrewsbury*
30902	*Wellington*		30922	*Marlborough*
30903	*Charterhouse*		30923	*Bradfield*
30904	*Lancing*		30924	*Haileybury*
30905	*Tonbridge*		30925	*Cheltenham*
30906	*Sherborne*		30926	*Repton*
30907	*Dulwich*		30927	*Clifton*
30908	*Westminster*		30928	*Stowe*
30909	*St. Paul's*		30929	*Malvern*
30910	*Merchant Taylors*		30930	*Radley*
30911	*Dover*		30931	*King's Wimbledon*
30912	*Downside*		30932	*Blundells*
30913	*Christ's Hospital*		30933	*King's Canterbury*
30914	*Eastbourne*		30934	*St. Lawrence*
30915	*Brighton*		30935	*Sevenoaks*
30916	*Whitgift*		30936	*Cranleigh*
30917	*Ardingly*		30937	*Epsom*
30918	*Hurstpierpoint*		30938	*St Olave's*
30919	*Harrow*		30939	*Leatherhead*

The first example of this forty-strong class was completed at Eastleigh Works in March 1930 and the last in July 1935. These powerful engines were to be found at many locations on the Southern Region. The appearance of several members of the class was considerably altered by the fitting from 1938 onwards of multiple jet blastpipes and large chimneys. All were withdrawn during 1961/2. Fortunately three have survived.

'Schools' class no. 30907 *Dulwich* at Bricklayer's Arms depot. This engine was one of the batch of ten allocated to St Leonards. Note the large chimney fitted.

23.11.54

'Schools' class no. 30932 *Blundells* at Ramsgate. This was a Stewarts Lane engine and was ready to work back to London. Note the signs of hard running on the smokebox door.

6.7.53

'Schools' class no. 30925 *Cheltenham* at Stewarts Lane depot. This engine was completed in April 1934 and withdrawn in December 1962 having run a total of 1,127,788 miles. This member of the forty-strong class was one of the three to survive and is now part of the National Collection.

23.11.54

K class 2–6–0 4MT

Designer: L.B. Billinton.
Total built: 17, British Railway number series 32337–53.

Principal dimensions

Weight:	Locomotive	63 tons 15 cwt
Boiler Pressure:		180 lb/sq in (superheated)
Driving Wheels:		5 ft 6 in
Tractive Effort:		26,580 lb
Cylinders:		(0) 21 in x 26 in

The Southern Region had seventeen of these useful 2–6–0s originating from the London, Brighton & South Coast Railway and introduced in 1913. During the fifties the majority of these locomotives were to be found allocated to Three Bridges depot. None has survived into preservation.

Three Bridges depot was the home shed for the majority of the K class in the fifties with engines from there working to Brighton and elsewhere. No. 32344 stands alongside the coaling stage. Note the Westinghouse pump fitted in front of the cab.

25.6.55

K class no. 32345 turns at Brighton shed. This engine was one of the Three Bridges allocation. This class was first introduced in 1913 but unfortunately none has survived.

14.7.54

126

N class 2–6–0 4MT

Designer: R.E.L. Maunsell.
Total built: N – 80, N1 – 6.

Principal dimensions	**N**	**N1**
Weight:	61 tons 4 cwt	64 tons 5 cwt
Boiler Pressure:	200 lb/sq in (superheated)	200 lb/sq in (superheated)
Driving Wheels:	5 ft 6 in	5 ft 6 in
Tractive Effort:	26,035 lb	27,695 lb
Cylinders:	(0) 19 in x 28 in	(3) 16 in x 28 in

Walschaerts valve gear – piston valves.

The Southern Region operated a sizeable fleet of mixed traffic 2–6–0 locomotives comprising several classes. Among them were eighty N class locomotives and six of the three cylinder N1 class. The first of the very useful N class made its appearance in 1917 to the design of Maunsell for the South Eastern & Chatham Railway. Fifty locomotives were built for the Southern Railway at Woolwich Arsenal and a further batch of fifteen locomotives were constructed in 1932–4. The latter had modified tenders and were numbered 31400–14.

The first of the six N1 three cylinder engines was constructed in 1922, to be followed by five more in 1930.

Only one member of these classes has survived into preservation. This is no. 31874, built at Woolwich Arsenal in 1925, which is to be found at the Mid-Hants Railway.

N class no. 31819 was one of the Ashford-built locomotives completed in May 1922. Here it is just departing from Dover shed ready for its next turn of duty.

3.7.53

The N class no. 31838 was an Exmouth Junction locomotive which had just received attention at Ashford Works. This locomotive was built there in July 1924.

14.5.55

U and U1 class 2–6–0 4MT

Designer: R.E.L. Maunsell.
Total built: 71.

Principal dimensions

Weight:	Locomotive	63 tons
Boiler Pressure:		200 lb/sq in (superheated)
Driving Wheels:		6 ft
Tractive Effort:	U class	23,865 lb
	U1 class	25,385 lb
Cylinders:	U class	(0) 19 in x 28 in
	U1 class	(3) 16 in x 28 in

Walschaerts valve gear – piston valve.

The first of the very useful U class locomotives appeared in 1928, delivered in two batches. The first batch were rebuilds from the ill-fated SECR 'River' class 2–6–4Ts introduced in 1917, which resulted from the Sevenoaks derailment of one of these engines at high speed in 1927. The second batch were new locomotives with smaller splashers and detail alterations. Both were two cylinder engines. The U1 class were three cylinder locomotives. No. 31890 was a conversion from a 2–6–4T and the rest were a new construction built in 1931–2 having minor differences to the prototype. These engines were widespread throughout the Southern Region, U and U1 totalling seventy-one locomotives.

Four examples of the U class survive including no. 31806 which was formerly 2–6–4T *River Torridge*.

This member of the U class, no. 31806, seen here leaving Eastleigh, is one of the batch rebuilt from the 'River' class 2–6–4Ts, in this case *River Torridge*. This engine has survived into preservation and is to be found on the Mid-Hants Railway which is known as the Watercress Line.

9.11.55

Another of the rebuilds is no. 31804, seen here at Exmouth Junction shed. These were two cylinder engines first introduced in 1928, the year after the high speed derailment of the 2–6–4T 'River' class locomotive. No. 31804 was rebuilt at Brighton works in June 1928.

4.9.56

U class no. 31637 was one of the batch of new construction with smaller splashers and other detail alterations. The engine had just arrived at Dover shed when this picture was taken.

3.7.53

Fresh from overhaul at Ashford Works, no. 31628 stands in the yard awaiting towing to the running shed where it would be coaled and watered and undertake running-in trials.

14.5.55

The three cylinder U1 introduced in 1928 had straight running plates and other detail differences. No. 31898 is seen at Ashford shed. This was one of several U1 class allocated to Redhill at the time.
1.7.55

C class 0–6–0 3F

Designer: H.S. Wainwright.
Total built: 109.

Principal dimensions

Weight:	Locomotive	43 tons 16 cwt
Boiler Pressure:		160 lb/sq in
Driving Wheels:		5 ft 2 in
Tractive Effort:		19,520 lb
Cylinders:		18½ in x 26 in
Stephenson valve gear.		

This was the largest of the 0–6–0 classes to be found on the Southern Region, with examples allocated to many depots. The very useful C class was introduced to the South Eastern & Chatham Railway by Wainwright in 1900. One was rebuilt to a 0–6–0ST in 1917 and lasted until 1951. Two were withdrawn in Southern days but the rest were taken over by British Railways. Their numbers were slowly whittled away during the fifties but over forty were still active in 1960 and it was not until July 1963 that the last member of the class was withdrawn. Just one survives today, no. 31592, built at Longhedge in 1902, which is now to be found on the Bluebell Railway.

Fresh from what was probably its last general overhaul, no. 31691 gets a quick check over from its driver at Stewarts Lane. This member of the C class was a Gillingham locomotive in its final years. It was withdrawn from service in February 1959 and cut up the following month at Ashford Works.

1.11.51

The numbering of the C class did not follow any pattern. No. 31498 was a Hither Green engine seen here at Ashford depot, coaled and watered ready to work home. No. 31498 survived in service until July 1961.

14.5.55

Hither Green depot had a large allocation of goods locomotives used on inter-regional freights, local work and shunting duties. No. 31510 simmers in the sunshine awaiting its next duty. The engine was among the last in normal service and was withdrawn in June 1962.

24.5.56

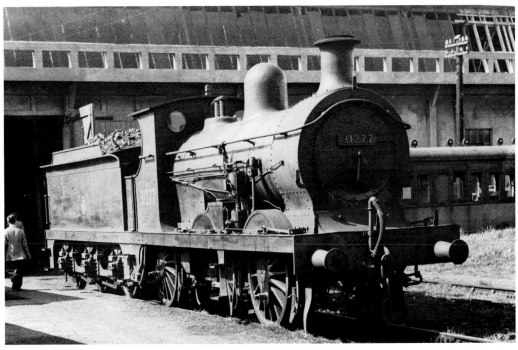

C class no. 31277 receiving attention at Hither Green, the middle pair of driving wheels having been removed. Note the old coach body in use as a store on the right hand side of the picture.

14.5.55

Many examples of the C class were to be found in the London area during the fifties. No. 31508, having visited the coaling plant, replenishes its water supply prior to leaving Stewarts Lane depot. This member of the class was withdrawn in September 1957.

1.11.51

C2X class 0–6–0 3F

Designer: D.E. Marsh.
Total built: 45.

Principal dimensions

Weight:	Locomotive	45 tons 5 cwt
Boiler Pressure:		170 lb/sq in
Driving Wheels:		5 ft
Tractive Effort:		19,175 lb
Cylinders:		17½ in x 26 in

Commonly known as 'Vulcans', the C2Xs were rebuilds of the C2 class which consisted of fifty-five locomotives. The majority of these were rebuilt with larger boilers and extended smokeboxes and reclassified C2X. The C2s were built by Vulcan Foundry, hence their common name. The C2X was a design by D.E. Marsh, Chief Mechanical Engineer of the London Brighton & South Coast Railway, and was introduced in 1908. Forty-five C2Xs were taken over by British Railways and withdrawals commenced in 1957 with the last two survivors going in February 1962. All the members of the class ended their days at Ashford Works.

Fresh from Works overhaul at Ashford, C2X no. 32551 was coaled and ready to return to its home shed, Bricklayers Arms. This engine was one of those fitted with a second top feed dome although it had been unused for some years. This engine remained in service for five more years, being withdrawn in February 1960.

14.5.55

Ex-works from Ashford after light repairs, C2X no. 32528 had acquired a fully repainted tender. This engine was one with the single dome. No. 32528 was withdrawn in March 1961 and cut up at Ashford Works.

14.5.55

Several examples of the C2X class were to be found at Bricklayers Arms depot including no. 32553, an example with the second dome. This locomotive was to remain in service until August 1961 when, like its classmates, it ended its days at Ashford Works.

1.11.51

O1 class 0–6–0 1F

Designer: H.S. Wainwright.
Total built: 58.

Principal dimensions

Weight:	Locomotive	41 tons 1 cwt
Boiler Pressure:		150 lb/sq in
Driving Wheels:		5 ft 2 in
Tractive Effort:		17,325 lb
Cylinders:		18 in x 26 in

Stephenson valve gear.

Fifty-five members of the O1 class were taken into British Railways stock, three of which had earlier been sold to the East Kent Railway. These engines were rebuilds of the Stirling O class 0–6–0s first introduced in 1878. Rebuilding commenced in 1903 to the design of Wainwright and included domed boiler and new cab. The class was easily distinguished by the outside frame tenders. Withdrawals were rapid during the first few years after nationalization. In the mid-fifties just eight remained in service, mostly used on local goods and shunting work and the last survivor, no. 31065, was withdrawn in June 1961. This engine was built at Ashford in 1896 and rebuilt in 1908 and fortunately still survives.

O1 class no. 31425 was employed on shed pilot duties at Dover. This engine was withdrawn in August 1959 and after three months stored at Ashford Works it was cut up there in November 1959.

3.7.53

The fireman of O1 class no. 31064 takes the opportunity of damping down the coal as the locomotive waits to leave Ashford shed. This engine was withdrawn from Stewarts Lane in May 1958 and on arrival at Ashford Works was cut up almost immediately.

14.5.55

Another picture of no. 31064 shows clearly the unusual outside frame tender fitted to the O1s. Up until the closure of the Kent & East Sussex Railway, an Ashford O1 was normally to be found working the first section of the line.

14.5.55

The Kent & East Sussex passenger train stands at Headcorn with an O1 ready to work the section to Rolvendon. Ashford shed had an allocation of three O1s which took their turn on this duty.

4.7.53

Q class 0–6–0 4F

Designer: R.E.L. Maunsell.
Total built: 20, BR number series 30530–49.

Principal dimensions

Weight:	Locomotive	49 tons 10 cwt
Boiler Pressure:		200 lb/sq in (superheated)
Driving Wheels:		5 ft 1 in
Tractive Effort:		26,160 lb
Cylinders:		19 in x 26 in

Stephenson valve gear – piston valves.

The first of this twenty-strong class designed by Maunsell was completed at Eastleigh in January 1938 with the last emerging in September 1939. Several of these engines were later fitted with multiple jet blastpipes and large chimneys which considerably altered their outward appearance. The class was to remain intact until November 1962 when no. 30540 was withdrawn. Massive inroads were made in 1963/4 until only nos. 30535/45 remained in service in 1965 with the latter being the last survivor. It was withdrawn in May 1965. One member of the class was to end up at Barry and after several years was rescued for preservation and is now to be found on the Bluebell Railway.

Several members of the twenty-strong Q class were allocated to Eastleigh, including no. 30536, seen here at its home shed. The large chimneys and multiple jet blastpipes were fitted to a number of the class and no. 30536 was so altered in 1947.

8.11.55

Q1 class 0–6–0 5F

Designer: O.V. Bulleid.
Total built: 40, BR number series 33001–40.

Principal dimensions

Weight:	Locomotive	51 tons 5 cwt
Boiler Pressure:		230 lb/sq in (superheated)
Driving Wheels:		5 ft 1 in
Tractive Effort:		30,080 lb
Cylinders:		19 in x 26 in

Stephenson valve gear – piston valves.

The appearance of the first Q1 class locomotive with its unusual design provoked much discussion and comment. These engines were introduced by Bulleid in 1942 and were a powerful 'Austerity' design needed to handle the ever increasing wartime goods traffic. One member of the class, no. 33001, built at Brighton in 1942, has survived as part of the National Collection.

The Q1 class was an 'Austerity' design introduced in 1942. No. 33019, a Guildford engine, is seen here in the Works yard at Ashford.

14.5.55

Although officially withdrawn in January 1966, Q1 no. 33006 was still active for several more months. When photographed it was engaged in carriage shunting at Eastleigh Works. It also worked a rail tour in April 1966 before ending its days at Cashmores in August of the same year.

26.3.66

700 class 0–6–0 4F

Designer: D. Drummond.
Total built: 30.

Principal dimensions

Weight:	Locomotive	46 tons 14 cwt
Boiler Pressure:		180 lb/sq in (superheated)
Driving Wheels:		5 ft 1 in
Tractive Effort:		23,540 lb
Cylinders:		19 in x 26 in

Many famous locomotive designs were to acquire common names. The 700 class locomotives designed by Drummond for the London & South Western Railway were widely known as 'Black Motors'. The first member of the thirty-strong class was completed in March 1897, the same company building all the class in that same year. In later years all were superheated. While designed for goods work the 700 class locomotives were occasionally used on specials and excursion trains. All survived to be taken into Southern Region stock. Withdrawals commenced in September 1957 with no. 30688 from Feltham depot. Massive inroads into the class took place in 1961/2 and it became extinct in December of that year. Unfortunately none has survived.

Fresh from Works overhaul no. 30701 stands outside Feltham shed. This engine was built by Dubs & Co in May 1897 and it remained in service until July 1961. It was a Nine Elms engine throughout the fifties and ended its days at Eastleigh Works.

12.7.54

0395 class 0–6–0 1F

Designer: W. Adams.

Principal dimensions

Weight:	Locomotive	37 tons 12 cwt
Boiler Pressure:		140 lb/sq in
Driving Wheels:		5 ft 1 in
Tractive Effort:		15,535 lb
Cylinders:		17½ in x 26 in

Only a small number of these 0–6–0s remained in service at the end of 1955. They were designed by Adams for the London & South Western Railway and first made their appearance in 1881. A large number of the class were sent to the Middle East and elsewhere during the First World War. Those that remained in traffic consisted of a number of variations but all were built by Neilson & Co. The 0395 class were used on light duties in their later years and none has survived into preservation.

No. 30568 is pictured at its home depot of Feltham. This engine was an example of the original Adams LSWR design and it remained in service until April 1958.

12.7.54

The 0395 class was a familiar sight on light duties in the Woking and Wimbledon areas during the mid-fifties. This picture of no. 30568 shows clearly the rather open cab fitted to these locomotives and the Neilson Co. works plate on the middle splasher.

12.7.54

G16 class 4–8–0T 7F

Designer: R.W. Urie.
Total built: 4, BR number series 30492–5.

Principal dimensions

Weight:	95 tons 2 cwt
Boiler Pressure:	180 lb/sq in (superheated)
Driving Wheels:	5 ft 1 in
Tractive Effort:	33,990 lb
Cylinders:	(0) 22 in x 28 in

Walschaerts valve gear – piston valves.

Four of these large hump shunting tank locomotives were constructed at Eastleigh Works in 1921 for use at the then new marshalling yards at Feltham. The engines were to the design of Urie for the London & South Western Railway. All survived into British Railways stock. Two members of the class were withdrawn in 1959 and the remaining two in December 1962. All ended their days at Eastleigh Works.

No. 30493, photographed at Feltham depot, was out of use and standing on an isolated siding. This locomotive was one of the first two withdrawn. After being condemned in December 1959, it was cut up at Eastleigh Works in January 1960.

12.7.54

H16 class 4–6–2T 5F

Designer: R.W. Urie.
Total built: 5.

Principal dimensions

Weight:	96 tons 8 cwt
Boiler Pressure:	180 lb/sq in (superheated)
Driving Wheels:	5 ft 7 in
Tractive Effort:	28,200 lb
Cylinders:	(O) 21 in x 28 in

Walschaerts valve gear – piston valves.

This class of five locomotives was originally intended for interchange goods traffic. Designed by Urie for the London & South Western Railway, the first example was completed at Eastleigh in November 1921. During the fifties the entire class was to be found operating from Feltham shed working on shunting duties, local goods and occasional empty stock workings. In their final years several were used on Fawley branch oil trains. Four were withdrawn in November 1962 and no. 30517 the following month. All were cut up.

The last example of the class in service, no. 30517, was employed twice on part of a rail tour in its final weeks of service.

No. 30517, seen here at Feltham MPD, was to be the last of this five-strong class in service. It was withdrawn in December 1962. During its last weeks this engine performed well on rail tours covering the South London area.

12.7.54

W class 2–6–4T 5F

Designer: R.E.L. Maunsell.
Total built: 15, BR number series 31911–25.

Principal dimensions

Weight:	90 tons 14 cwt
Boiler Pressure:	200 lb/sq in (superheated)
Driving Wheels:	5 ft 6 in
Tractive Effort:	29,450 lb
Cylinders:	(3) 16½ in x 28 in

Walschaerts valve gear – piston valves.

The W class made its first appearance in 1931 as a development of the N1 class 2–6–0. The design was introduced by Maunsell for the Southern Railway. These engines included some parts from the earlier 'River' class tanks and were designed for freight work. The majority of the class of fifteen locomotives was allocated to the London area with a considerable number based at Hither Green where their duties included inter-regional freights. Several of these locomotives were to end their days at Cohens Scrapyard, Kettering, and none has survived into preservation.

At the time of my visit to Hither Green I found three of the W class 2–6–4 tanks in the shed yard awaiting their next duty. Eight members of the class were allocated to the depot including the one in this picture, no. 31922.

24.5.56

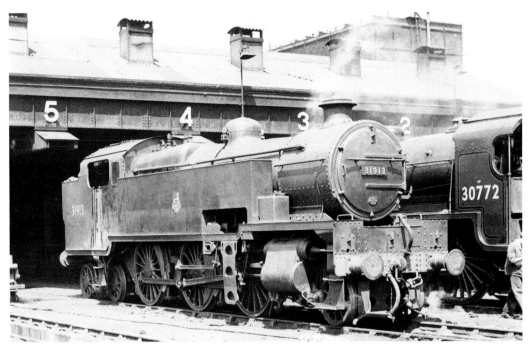

W class no. 31913 at Hither Green shed in company with 'King Arthur' class no. 30772 *Sir Percivale.* The W class was a familiar sight at Hither Green as the majority of the class was allocated to this depot.

24.5.56

The Hither Green W class tanks were usually maintained in good external condition as can be seen from this picture of no. 31923. This very pleasing design was confined to freight work and those at Hither Green often hauled inter-regional freight.

24.5.56

Z class 0–8–0T 7F

Designer: R.E.L. Maunsell.
Total built: 8, BR number series 30950–7.

Principal dimensions

Weight:	71 tons 12 cwt
Boiler Pressure:	180 lb/sq in
Driving Wheels:	4 ft 8 in
Tractive Effort:	29,375 lb
Cylinders:	(3) 16 in x 18 in

Walschaerts valve gear – piston valves.

This wheel arrangement for tank locomotives was never common on British Railways and the Southern Region had just eight locomotives comprising the Z class. All were built in 1929 at Brighton Works to the design of Maunsell for the Southern Railway.

During the fifties members of this class were to be found at several depots, Exmouth Junction, Three Bridges and Brighton among them. They were powerful, well liked engines ideal for heavy shunting and banking duties. All eight engines were withdrawn during 1962 and none has survived into preservation.

One member of the Z class was usually employed on shunting duties at Exmouth Junction. No. 30950 was the first engine of the class to be completed at Brighton Works in March 1929.

4.9.56

The almost side view of no. 30950 illustrates clearly the considerable overhang of the front and rear of Z class locomotives. These engines were well liked by their crews, not least for their roomy, comfortable cabs.

4.9.56

0415 class 4–4–2T 1P

Designer: W. Adams.
Total built: 72.

Principal dimensions

Weight:	55 tons 2 cwt
Boiler Pressure:	160 lb/sq in
Driving Wheels:	5 ft 7 in
Tractive Effort:	14,920 lb
Cylinders:	(0) 17½ in x 24 in

Stephenson valve gear.

During the fifties the graceful Adams 4–4–2Ts were still to be found at work on the Lyme Regis branch attracting many enthusiasts, especially on summer Saturdays when a pair of these locomotives could be seen double-heading. The surviving three engines of this class were all built by different companies in 1885: no. 30582 by R. Stephenson, no. 30583 by Neilson & Co., and no. 30584 by Dubs & Co. One of these engines, LSWR no. 488 (no. 30583), was sold in 1917 and later passed into the ownership of the East Kent Railway from where it was repurchased by the Southern Railway in 1946. This is the only survivor of the trio and is to be found on the Bluebell Railway.

Adams 'Radial tank' no. 30582 backs onto the Lyme Regis branch train at Axminster. This engine was one of those built by R. Stephenson and it remained in service until July 1961.

3.9.56

The Lyme Regis branch attracted enthusiasts from a wide area. No. 30582 was the branch locomotive at the time of my visit and is seen here at Axminster station. The elegant lines of this class can be appreciated from this photograph. The 0415 carried fully lined black livery.

3.9.56

E1/R class 0–6–2T 2MT

Designer: R.E.L. Maunsell.
Total built: 10.

Principal dimensions

Weight:	50 tons 5 cwt
Boiler Pressure:	170 lb/sq in
Driving Wheels:	4 ft 6 in
Tractive Effort:	18,560 lb
Cylinders:	17 in x 24 in

The ten engines comprising this class were rebuilds of the Stroudley E1 class 0–6–0Ts introduced in 1874. Rebuilding of these locomotives took place in 1927/8 when they were fitted with a trailing axle and large bunker. During the fifties they were to be found at Exmouth Junction, Plymouth Friary and Barnstaple and were used principally for handling passenger services. The last example was withdrawn in 1959.

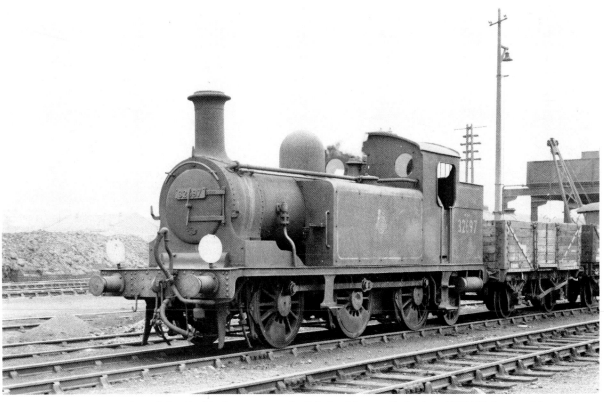

The ten examples of the E1/R class were rebuilds by Maunsell during 1927/28 for working passenger services in the West Country. In this picture no. 32697 was on more mundane duties as shed pilot at Exmouth Junction depot.

4.9.56

E3 class 0–6–2T 2MT

Designer: R.J. Billinton.
Total built: 16.

Principal dimensions

Weight:	56 tons 10 cwt
Boiler Pressure:	160 lb/sq in and 170 lb/sq in
Driving Wheels:	4 ft 6 in
Tractive Effort:	20,055 lb and 21,305 lb
Cylinders:	17½ in x 26 in

These locomotives were designed by R.J. Billinton for the London Brighton & South Coast Railway and were introduced in 1894. From 1918 onwards they were reboilered, fitted with an extended smokebox and the cylinder diameter was reduced. There were also variations of boiler fittings on these locomotives. Fifteen examples were in service in the fifties and the last engine remained until 1959.

No. 32458 awaits attention at Bricklayers Arms. This engine was one of those with enclosed safety valves and larger dome. Many of the smaller locomotive repairs were carried out at Bricklayers Arms.

25.11.54

E3 no. 32167 has received the attention of the cleaners at Brighton shed. This engine was fitted with the smaller dome and open type Ramsbottom safety valves. The E3s were mostly used on freight and shunting duties.

25.6.55

The E3 class consisted of just fifteen locomotives during the fifties. No. 32166 was photographed as it was about to leave Stewarts Lane depot. This engine was fitted with one of the smaller domes and in this view the rather battered Westinghouse pump can be clearly seen. Note also the two lamps at the rear.

1.11.51

E4 class 0–6–2T 2MT

Designer: R.J. Billinton.
Total built: 75.

Principal dimensions

Weight:	57 tons 10 cwt
Boiler Pressure:	170 lb/sq in
Driving Wheels:	5 ft
Tractive Effort:	19,175 lb
Cylinders:	$17\frac{1}{2}$ in x 26 in

Stephenson valve gear.

The E4 class locomotives were to be found at many Southern Region depots during the fifties and several examples were allocated to Nine Elms depot. These engines were introduced by R.J. Billinton in 1910, being a development of the earlier E3 class. They were useful locomotives employed on passenger work and many other duties. All survived to be taken into BR stock with one exception which was cut up in 1944. Four of the class were reboilered to become E4X class in 1909–12 and the last of these was withdrawn in 1959. Fortunately one, no. 32473, survived the cutter's torch and has been preserved on the Bluebell Railway for many years, still carrying its former LBSCR name *Birch Grove*.

Fresh from Works overhaul at Ashford E4 no. 32556 was in unlined black livery. The E4s were to be found at many depots during the fifties on a wide range of duties.

1.7.53

E4 no. 32580 at Ashford shed finished in lined out black livery which the majority of the class carried. This was a Tonbridge engine and may have possibly visited the nearby works for light repairs itself or towing a locomotive due for repair.

14.5.55

E5 class 0–6–2T 2MT

Designer: R.J. Billinton.
Total built: 30.

Principal dimensions

Weight:	60 tons
Boiler Pressure:	160 lb/sq in
Driving Wheels:	5 ft 6 in
Tractive Effort:	16,410 lb
Cylinders:	17½ in x 26 in

Development of the E4 class resulted in the E5 class, introduced by R.J. Billinton in 1902 with thirty examples built for passenger work over a two year period. They were all withdrawn by 1956 including the four engines reboilered and classified E5X.

155

E5 class no. 32593 at Dover shed. Note the typical tapered chimney fitted to this class. All the E5s and E5X rebuilds were withdrawn by 1956.

3.7.53

E6 class 0–6–2T 4F

Designer: R.J. Billinton.
Total built: 12.

Principal dimensions	E6	E6X
Weight:	61 tons	63 tons
Boiler Pressure:	160 lb/sq in	170 lb/sq in
Driving Wheels:	4 ft 6 in	4 ft 6 in
Tractive Effort:	21,215 lb	22,540 lb
Cylinders:	18 in x 26 in	18 in x 26 in

In 1904 R.J. Billinton introduced his E6 class, which was a development of the E5 with smaller wheels, for freight work. In 1911 two engines were reboilered with larger C3 type boilers and reclassified E6X. The last of the E6s were withdrawn in 1961 with the two rebuilds going in 1957 and 1959.

The E6 class was designed principally for freight work and introduced in 1904. No. 32412 was photographed at Ashford. The E6 class became extinct in 1961.

14.5.55

Two of the E6 class were rebuilt with C3 type boilers in 1911 and reclassified E6X. No. 32407 and sister engine no. 32411 were both allocated to Norwood Junction depot (75C). No. 32407 is seen here on a visit to Ashford.

14.5.55

A1X class 0–6–0T 0P

Designer: W. Stroudley.

Principal dimensions

Weight:	28 tons 5 cwt
Boiler Pressure:	150 lb/sq in
Driving Wheels:	4 ft
Tractive Effort:	7,650 lb
Cylinders:	12 in x 20 in

Stephenson valve gear.
One locomotive, no. 32636, had a larger cylinder size and higher tractive effort.

The famous 'Terriers' introduced by Stroudley for the London Brighton & South Coast Railway in 1872 were all built at Brighton Works. The A1X class consisted of rebuilds of these engines and first appeared in 1911 with Marsh boilers and extended smokeboxes. Locomotives of this class were responsible for working the Hayling Island branch and other light duties. No. 2635 was repainted in LBSCR yellow livery in 1946 and renumbered 377S for use at Brighton Works and remained in this condition until 1959 when it was transferred back to normal stock and reverted to its old number, 32635. Fortunately eight A1Xs still survive in preservation in the British Isles as well as DS680 and A1 which are to be found in Canada.

In 1946 no. 2635 was repainted in yellow LBSCR livery, lettered *Brighton Works* and numbered 377S for shunting duties at the Works where it was photographed. In 1959 it was transferred back to capital stock and renumbered 32635. This engine still survives as no. 72 *Fenchurch* on the Bluebell Railway.

14.7.54

Another lucky survivor is no. 32655 (no. 55 *Stepney* on the Bluebell Railway). The engine is seen here ready to depart with a Kent & East Sussex train at Rolvendon. This engine was originally built in 1875 and later rebuilt.

4.7.53

E1 class 0–6–0T 2F

Designer: W. Stroudley.
Total built: 80.

Principal dimensions

Weight:	44 tons 3 cwt
Boiler Pressure:	170 lb/sq in
Driving Wheels:	4 ft 6 in
Tractive Effort:	18,560 lb
Cylinders:	17 in x 24 in

Stephenson valve gear.

Eighty examples of the E1 class were built to the design of Stroudley for the London Brighton & South Coast Railway between 1874 and 1883. They were later reboiled by Marsh. Quite a number survived to be taken into British Railways stock and four of these, nos. W1–4 (*Medina*, *Yarmouth*, *Ryde* and *Wroxall* respectively), were used on the Isle of Wight. The last example of the class was withdrawn in 1961. One example still survives, having been sold out of service many years previously. The engine worked at the National Coal Board Rawnsley Colliery in Staffordshire and it is now preserved at the East Somerset Railway.

Several members of the E1 class were employed on shunting work at Southampton docks. No. 32113 is seen there with Italian ferry wagons. During the fifties the docks had their own depot, shedcode 71I, and among the sixteen locomotives allocated were two E1s, the others being USA class 0–6–0Ts.

9.11.55

The other E1 shunting at the docks at the time of my visit was no. 32606. Several of the USA class tanks especially purchased by the Southern Railway were also busy in the area.

9.11.55

E2 class 0–6–0T 3F

Designer: L.B. Billinton.
Total built: 10, BR number series 32100–9.

Principal dimensions

Weight:	52 tons 15 cwt (53 tons 10 cwt with extended tanks)
Boiler Pressure:	170 lb/sq in
Driving Wheels:	4 ft 6 in
Tractive Effort:	21,305 lb
Cylinders:	17½ in x 26 in

This design was introduced by L.B. Billinton for the London Brighton & South Coast Railway in 1913 and all were constructed within a three year period. The last five members of the class, which appeared from 1915 onwards, were built with side tanks extended further forward. During the fifties the majority were allocated to Stewarts Lane depot and the other members of the class were at Dover. All ten were scrapped.

E2 class no. 32105 is busily engaged on shunting work at Stewarts Lane. Eight members of the class were allocated here during the fifties.

1.11.51

E2 class no. 32107 was one of the class with extended tanks which can be clearly seen in this picture taken at Stewarts Lane. Note that the locomotive had not received the British Railways emblem and the word Southern can be clearly seen as can the number 7 of 2107 which it would have carried in those days.

1.11.51

G6 class 0–6–0T 2F

Designer: W. Adams.

Principal dimensions

Weight:	47 tons 13 cwt
Boiler Pressure:	160 lb/sq in
Driving Wheels:	4 ft 10 in
Tractive Effort:	17,235 lb
Cylinders:	$17\frac{1}{2}$ in x 24 in

The G6 class made its first appearance in 1894 to Adams's design for the London & South Western Railway. The few examples in service during the fifties were widely scattered with one being in Departmental stock. None has survived into preservation.

Busily shunting near Eastleigh Station was G6 class no. 30162. The few remaining examples were to be found scattered over a wide area at this time.

8.11.55

P class 0–6–0T 0F

Designer: H.S. Wainwright.

Principal dimensions

Weight:	28 tons 10 cwt
Boiler Pressure:	160 lb/sq in
Driving Wheels:	3 ft 9⅛ in
Tractive Effort:	7,810 lb
Cylinders:	12 in x 18 in

These small tank locomotives were originally introduced for push-pull work and first appeared in 1909 to a design by Wainwright. They were built at Ashford Works for the South Eastern & Chatham Railway. Later, they were used for light shunting work.

The eight members of the class in BR days were widely spread. Two were to be found at Stewarts Lane with others at Dover, Eastleigh and Brighton. One member of the class, no. 31178, was sold to Bowaters Paper Mills at Sittingbourne, Kent, where it became *Pioneer II* and no. 31556 was sold to James Hodson (Millers) Ltd of Robertsbridge and named *Pride of Sussex*. Both locomotives have survived into preservation together with two other members of the class, nos. 31027 and 31323.

P class no. 31556 was employed as shed pilot at Brighton. The engine was built in 1909 and has survived into preservation at the present time on the Kent & East Sussex Railway. Note the rather cramped cab conditions on these locomotives. This engine was sold by BR to James Hodson (Millers) Ltd, Robertsbridge, and named *Pride of Sussex*.

14.7.54

P class no. 31557 shunting at Stewarts Lane. Usually two members of the class were allocated to this depot although only one was to be found in daily use during the early fifties. This particular engine is not one of the survivors.

1.11.51

This P class 0–6–0T was formerly British Railways no. 31178 built at Ashford Works in 1910. It was sold for industrial use to Bowaters United Kingdom Pulp & Paper Mills Ltd, Sittingbourne, Kent, where it was named *Pioneer II* and where this picture was taken. Fortunately, this locomotive has survived into preservation and is to be seen on the Bluebell Railway.

10.6.67

No. 31178 is seen here at Eastleigh before it was sold for further service on the industrial railway system at Bowaters, Sittingbourne.

8.11.55

R1 class 0–6–0T 2F

Designer: J. Stirling.

Principal dimensions

Weight:	46 tons
Boiler Pressure:	160 lb/sq in
Driving Wheels:	5 ft 2 in (others were fitted with 5 ft 1 in)
Tractive Effort:	18,480 lb
Cylinders:	18 in x 26 in

Many readers will recall members of this class during the fifties handling the boat trains from Folkestone Junction to the Harbour station and back. Quite often four locomotives would be required to work a train up from the Harbour, three at the front and one banking, making a fine sight as they tackled the gradient. They were later replaced by Western Region pannier tanks. The R1 was introduced for the South Eastern Railway by Stirling in 1888. They were later rebuilt with domed boilers. Thirteen survived to be taken into BR stock and the last one was withdrawn in 1960.

Most of the class were allocated to Folkestone Junction and several were fitted with short Urie chimneys for use on the Whitstable branch. These retained the rounded Stirling cab. Unfortunately none has survived into preservation.

No. 31047 stands outside Folkestone Harbour shed awaiting its next duty. The locomotive is fitted with the later type cab. Seven of these engines were allocated to this shed in the fifties, comprising the shed's complete allocation. They worked the harbour branch and carriage duties.

6.7.53

Several R1 class locomotives were fitted with short Urie chimneys and retained the original round cab together with cut-down boiler mountings. These were used on the Whitstable branch and after its closure they could often be found towing engines between Ashford shed and Works. No. 31147 was on this duty when photographed.

14.5.55

Scenes such as this were a familiar sight at Folkestone Harbour in the fifties. Three R1 class 0–6–0Ts commence the climb to Folkestone Junction with a fourth banking. The leading engine is no. 31337 with nos. 31049 and 31069 assisting. The latter has the rounded Stirling type cab.

8.7.53

USA class 0–6–0T 3F

Designer: United States Army Transportation Corps.

Principal dimensions

Weight:	46 tons 10 cwt
Boiler Pressure:	210 lb/sq in
Driving Wheels:	4 ft 6 in
Tractive Effort:	21,600 lb
Cylinders:	(O) 16½ in x 24 in

Walschaerts valve gear – piston valves.

   This design was introduced in 1942 for the United States Army Transportation Corps. Fourteen of the engines were purchased by the Southern Railway in 1946 and fitted with modified cabs and bunkers for use at Southampton Docks. When taken over by British Railways they became nos. 30061–74. All were built by Vulcan except no. 30061 which was constructed by Porter.
   Withdrawals commenced in 1962 and six were transferred to Departmental stock including no. 30061 (DS233). Several of the Departmental engines were repainted in malachite green. Three of these locomotives have survived into preservation.

Six of the USA 0–6–0Ts were transferred to departmental service. No. 30061 became DS233 and was used at Redbridge Sleeper depot. This engine was the sole example of the Porter-built engines purchased and when constructed in 1942 it became WD no. 1264. It is seen here at Eastleigh, being withdrawn in 1967.

12.3.67

USA class no. 30072 stands in the shed yards at Southampton Dock depot. Note the damage to the tank sides. This engine has survived and was used to work the first train on the Keighley & Worth Valley line when it re-opened on 29 June 1968. It can still be found there.

9.11.55

USA class no. 30063 shunting at Southampton new docks. Note the duty no. 10 carried on the buffer beams. This engine was withdrawn in May 1962 following collision damage. This was one of the Vulcan locomotives constructed in 1942 and it entered Southern Railway service in October 1947.

9.11.55

D3 class 0–4–4T 1P

Designer: R.J. Billinton.
Total built: 36.

Principal dimensions

Weight:	52 tons
Boiler Pressure:	170 lb/sq in
Driving Wheels:	5 ft 6 in
Tractive Effort:	17,435 lb
Cylinders:	17½ in x 26 in

The D3 class originally consisted of thirty-six locomotives built between 1892 and 1896 but by the mid-fifties very few remained. The design was by R.J. Billinton for the London Brighton & South Coast Railway. They were later reboilered and from the mid-thirties fitted for push-pull working.

The last survivor of the D3 class was no. 32390, seen here at Brighton shed. These locomotives were push-pull fitted. No. 32390 was withdrawn during 1955.

14.7.54

H class 0–4–4T 1P

Designer: H.S. Wainwright.
Total built: 66.

Principal dimensions

Weight:	54 tons 8 cwt
Boiler Pressure:	160 lb/sq in
Driving Wheels:	5 ft 6 in
Tractive Effort:	17,360 lb
Cylinders:	18 in x 26 in

Stephenson valve gear.

    This class was designed by Wainwright for the South Eastern & Chatham Railway with the first example appearing in 1904. In all sixty-six locomotives were built, only two of which failed to become British Railways stock at nationalization. In 1949 the first of the class was fitted for push-pull working. The individual locomotive numbers were widely scattered.

    Only one member of the class has survived into preservation. No. 31263, which was built at Ashford in 1905, is now to be found on the Bluebell Railway.

H class no. 31521 is fresh from general overhaul at its home shed, Ashford. This locomotive was fitted for push-pull working and was resplendent in fully lined out black livery.

14.5.55

H class no. 31319 was one fitted for push-pull working. The equipment for this can be clearly seen in this picture taken at Stewarts Lane.

1.11.51

Bright as a new pin in fully lined out livery after a general overhaul at Ashford Works, H class no. 31306 was ready to return to its home depot, Gillingham (73D). These very useful 0–4–4Ts were to be found at several Southern Region depots. This engine was later fitted with push-pull equipment.

1.7.53

M7 class 0–4–4T 2P

Designer: D. Drummond.
Total built: 105.

Principal dimensions

Weight:	60 tons (62 tons for push-pull locomotives)
Boiler Pressure:	175 lb/sq in
Driving Wheels:	5 ft 7 in
Tractive Effort:	19,755 lb
Cylinders:	18½ in x 26 in

Stephenson valve gear.

The first of the large 0–4–4Ts of class M7 was completed in March 1897, the forerunner of a sizeable class of very useful locomotives. The design was by Drummond for the London & South Western Railway. Twenty-five locomotives were built the first year and there were to be several other orders until the final locomotive of the 105 built was completed in December 1911. All but one were taken into British Railways stock and one was withdrawn in 1948 following an accident. The remainder were left intact until withdrawals commenced in 1957.

There were several variations of the M7. In 1903 the first batch of engines with increased front overhang, steam reverser and other detail differences was built although these were not originally classified as M7. From 1925 a number of these locomotives were fitted for push-pull working. The class was widely used on branch lines in the south west. In the early sixties they were still to be found on the Swanage and Lymington branches. Other members of the class were to be found on station pilot and empty stock workings. Several were regularly seen at Clapham Junction on the latter duties at this time. The last of the M7s was withdrawn in May 1964. Two have survived into preservation, nos. 30053 and 30245, owned by the Swanage Railway and the National Railway Museum respectively. No. 30053 is one of the class fitted for push-pull working.

M7 class no. 30044 stands at Exmouth Junction shed. This locomotive is one of the original design built in March 1899 and it remained in service until August 1961. Several M7s were allocated to Exmouth Junction in the mid-fifties.

3.9.56

Fresh from light overhaul at Eastleigh Works and ready to return to its home depot, Nine Elms, no. 30243 was the second member of the class built and was completed in March 1897. Time was running out for the engine when this picture was taken as it was withdrawn in September 1958.

8.11.55

M7 no. 30323, one of the batch fitted with different front splashers, is seen here at Exmouth Junction. This M7 was completed in October 1900 and remained in service until December 1959.

4.9.56

M7 no. 30049 had just emerged from overhaul at Eastleigh Works and was in the process of having its tanks replenished. This was one of the engines fitted for push-pull working. Note the pump on the side of the smokebox and the compressed air reservoir under the front buffer. No. 30049 was a Horsham engine at this time.

8.11.55

O2 class 0–4–4T 1P

Designer: W. Adams for the London & South Western Railway in 1889.
Total built: 60.

Principal dimensions

Weight:	46 tons 18 cwt
Boiler Pressure:	160 lb/sq in
Driving Wheels:	4 ft 10 in
Tractive Effort:	17,235 lb
Cylinders:	17½ in x 24 in

Stephenson valve gear.

Sixty of these very useful locomotives were built between 1889 and 1895 at Nine Elms Works. Forty-eight engines remained in service at nationalization and of these twenty-five were on the mainland and twenty-three on the Isle of Wight. The last two O2s employed on the mainland were withdrawn in 1962. Several of the locomotives on the Isle of Wight remained in service for a number of years. Fortunately one of the class has survived into preservation, no. W24 *Calbourne*, built in 1891.

The engines used on the island were fitted with Westinghouse brakes and enlarged bunkers and all were named. Those which remained in service at the end of 1955 were:

W14	*Fishbourne*		W26	*Whitwell*
W15	*Cowes*		W27	*Merstone*
W16	*Ventnor*		W28	*Ashey*
W17	*Seaview*		W29	*Alverstone*
W18	*Ningwood*		W30	*Shorwell*
W20	*Shanklin*		W31	*Chale*
W21	*Sandown*		W32	*Bonchurch*
W22	*Brading*		W33	*Bembridge*
W24	*Calbourne*		W35	*Freshwater*
W25	*Godshill*		W36	*Carisbrooke*

O2 class no. 30177, the first member of the class built, was completed at Nine Elms Works in December 1889. The engine is seen here at Eastleigh Works. No. 30177 remained in service until October 1959.

8.11.55

O2 class no. W16 *Ventnor* is pictured at Ryde Esplanade station. The O2 class engines on the Isle of Wight were fitted with Westinghouse brakes and enlarged bunkers and all were named. One of these engines has survived into preservation, no. 24 *Calbourne*.

11.9.59

R class 0–4–4T 1P

Designer: J. Kirtley.

Principal dimensions

Weight:	48 tons 15 cwt
Boiler Pressure:	160 lb/sq in
Driving Wheels:	5 ft 6 in
Tractive Effort:	15,145 lb
Cylinders:	$17\frac{1}{2}$ in x 24 in

The R class was introduced by Kirtley for the London, Chatham & Dover Railway, the first example appearing in 1891. These were later rebuilt with H class boilers and a number were fitted for push-pull working. No. 31666, the last in service, was withdrawn in December 1955.

R class no. 31661 stands at Folkestone Junction shed. Note the 'SPL' plate on the bunker. This was a Dover engine and what the engine was doing at this shed is unknown, as Folkestone Junction's allocation was seven of the R1 class 0–6–0Ts only.

3.7.53

The last survivor of the R class, no. 31666 is seen at Tonbridge. This engine was fitted for push-pull working. The class became extinct when no. 31666 was withdrawn in December 1955.

1.7.53

0298 class 2–4–0WT 0F

Designer: J. Beattie.
Total built: 85.

Principal dimensions

Weight:	37 tons 16 cwt
Boiler Pressure:	160 lb/sq in
Driving Wheels:	5 ft 7 in
Tractive Effort:	11,050 lb
Cylinders:	(0) 16½ in x 20 in

Allan valve gear.

The three engines of this type which survived to be taken into British Railways stock long outlived their classmates. All were to be found at Wadebridge in Cornwall where they were retained for working the Wenford Bridge mineral line and local shunting duties. During the fifties two were normally in daily use with the third spare. Their British Railways numbers were 30585–87.

This design was first introduced by Beattie for the London & South Western Railway in 1874 and they were subsequently rebuilt and modified by Adams, Urie and Maunsell over the years. In their later years they were to provide a 'mecca' for railway enthusiasts as nothing like them was to be found elsewhere. The last survivors of the class other than these three were withdrawn in 1898! Unfortunately only two of these very unusual locomotives have survived into preservation.

179

This locomotive is the only one of the three Beattie 'Well' tanks not to survive. This engine was slightly different to its two classmates with rectangular splashers and the BR crest carried in front of the number as opposed to on the cab side. No. 30586 was on shunting duties at Wadebridge.

5.9.56

No. 30585 was originally built by Beyer Peacock in 1874 and rebuilt or modified on several occasions. After finishing its day's duties it was in the process of being coaled at Wadebridge.

5.9.56

The third engine of the trio was spare at the time of my visit and was in the small shed in company with an O2 class 0–4–4T. This engine is one of the two survivors. Wadebridge shed had an allocation of just five engines, the three 0298 class tanks and two O2 class tanks.

5.9.56

B4 class 0–4–0T 0F

Designer: W. Adams.

Principal dimensions

Weight:	33 tons 9 cwt (majority)
Boiler Pressure:	140 lb/sq in
Driving Wheels:	3 ft 9¾ in
Tractive Effort:	14,650 lb
Cylinders:	(0) 16 in x 22 in

There were several variations of the B4.

These sturdy small tank locomotives were designed by Adams for dock shunting and station pilot work. They were built in several batches with the first completed at Nine Elms Works in 1891. Most survived to be taken into British Railways stock but some were sold shortly afterwards and withdrawals proceeded apace until the last members of the class were withdrawn in 1963. These were nos. 30096 and 30102. The first was sold for private use to Southern Wharves Ltd where it acquired the name *Corrall Queen* although still running with front number and 71A plates. The second engine was sold to Butlins, restored and displayed at the Ayr holiday camp. Both locomotives still survive, the first on the Bluebell Railway and no. 30102 at Bressingham Steam Museum.

The B4 class had a long association with Southampton Docks until replaced by the USA tanks. During this time fourteen locomotives carried names but these were removed after the class ceased to be associated with the docks.

B4 class no. 30094 was completed in December 1892. When photographed at Plymouth Friary depot it had recently received a general overhaul. This side view illustrates clearly the short wheelbase of these locomotives. Note also the spark arrestor.

4.9.56

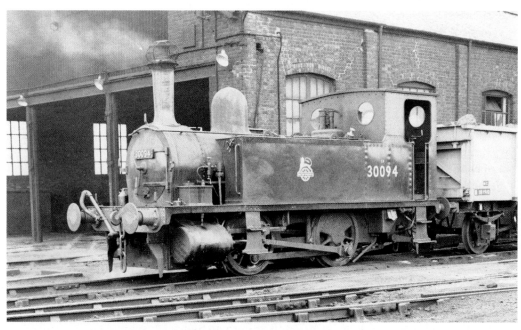

Another view of no. 30094 shows the rather battered cylinder casing more clearly. Four members of the class were allocated to Plymouth Friary depot. Despite the outwardly fine condition of this engine, it was withdrawn from service in March 1957.

4.9.56

B4 no. 30096 was withdrawn from service in October 1963 and later sold to Southern Wharves Ltd at Northam where this picture was taken. Note the nameplate *Corrall Queen* and the number and shed plates which it was still carrying from BR days. This engine still survives and is to be found on the Bluebell Railway.

12.3.67

C14 class 0–4–0T 0F

Designer: R.W. Urie.

Principal dimensions

Weight:	25 tons 15 cwt
Boiler Pressure:	150 lb/sq in
Driving Wheels:	3 ft
Tractive Effort:	9,720 lb
Cylinders:	(0) 14 in x 14 in

Walschaerts valve gear.
The C14 class locomotives were allocated to Eastleigh depot.

The locomotives of this class were rebuilds by Urie of the ten motor train 2–2–0Ts introduced by Drummond for the London & South Western Railway in 1906/7. Three of the rebuilds survived to be taken into British Railways stock at nationalization. One was in departmental stock numbered 77S and the other two engines were allocated nos. 30588/9. The latter survived until 1957 while no. 77S worked for a further two years before being withdrawn in April 1959 from Town Quay, Southampton, where the class had worked for many years.

C14 no. 30588 shunting on a wet Town Quay, Southampton. The C14s worked there for many years. This engine was withdrawn in 1957.

9.11.55

C14 no. 30589 stands at Eastleigh shed. The engine was used on a rail tour in 1952 over the Bishops Waltham branch. Note the taller B4 class chimney and absent tool boxes at the front of running plate.

8.11.55

Nameplates

The curved nameplate *Trevose Head* was carried by H2 class 'Brighton Atlantic' no. 32425.

The 'Battle of Britain' class locomotive nameplates had the words 'Battle of Britain Class' under the name and below this a plate with the Squadron crest where appropriate. *17 Squadron* was fitted to no. 34062, still in un-rebuilt form when this picture was taken.

'Merchant Navy' class no. 35004 *Cunard White Star*, photographed before the locomotive was rebuilt.

The 'Merchant Navy' nameplate *Holland–Afrika line* was carried by no. 35023 and was photographed on the locomotive in rebuilt form.